Elon Musk

The Biography of a Modern Genius and Business Titan

By Nate Whitman

Table of Content

Introduction

Elon Reeve Musk is a South African–born American technology entrepreneur, investor, and engineer. He became a multimillionaire early in his life following the sale of his start-up company Zip2. His net worth only grew from there, and in October 2018, Forbes listed him as the fifty-fourth-richest person in the world.

The businessman is best known for founding X.com, which subsequently became PayPal, SpaceX, Tesla Motors, and the Boring Company. He is also a co-founder of OpenAI, a nonprofit research company focused on promoting artificial intelligence, and Neuralink, a neurotechnology company that aims to develop interfaces for brain-computer interactions.

Elon Musk is a public figure with high goals, such as promoting the production and consumption of sustainable energy in order to reduce the consequences of global warming, and he is a space enthusiast with the dream of establishing a human colony on Mars. The billionaire is a well-known philanthropist with a golden heart that's eager to help whenever he can, and he has a very active social media presence, often sharing his opinions or engaging with other people through his Twitter account.

In spite of his good intention and overall charisma, Elon Musk has had his fair share of controversies. The mainstream media doesn't hold him in high regard and mostly focuses on his eccentricities and aloof character, going as far as conveniently ignoring circumstances or his good intentions.

Regardless of other's opinions on him, Elon Musk stays true to himself and his goals. He keeps being his genuine self no matter what and works hard to make his dreams a reality while also staying up to date to the latest news and internet sensations known as memes. His antics made him very popular with internet people who appreciate his open type of personality. Despite being a billionaire, he is a relatable human being that makes mistakes and enjoys a good laugh rather than sticking to a perfect persona.

He described his self-proclaimed life purpose as follows: "I would like to die thinking that humanity has a bright future. If we can solve sustainable energy and be well on our way to becoming a multi-planetary species with a self-sustaining civilization on another planet—to cope with a worst-case scenario happening and extinguishing human consciousness—then . . . I think that would be really good."[1]

One thing is clear: Elon Musk is set on changing the world for the better, and nothing can stop him.

---

[1] Ashlee Vance (2015), "Elon Musk: Tesla, SpaceX, and the Quest for a Fantastic Future," page 7.

Chapter 1: Early Life

Childhood

Elon Musk was born on June 28, 1971, in Pretoria, a city in the northern part of the Gauteng province in South Africa. He was named after his great-grandfather, John Elon Haldeman. His mother, Maye Musk, was a Canadian model and dietician while his father, Errol Musk, was a South African–born engineer, sailor, and pilot. They owned one of the biggest property in Pretoria as Errol business was very successful.

The Haldemans, Maye's side of the family, were peculiar people who dabbled in adventures. Scott Haldeman, Musk's father, reminisced about their childhood: "We were left with the impression that we were capable of anything. You just have to make a decision and do it. In that sense, my father would be very proud of Elon." Musk himself remembers fondly his grandmother and her stories about her early years: "My grandmother told these tales of how they almost died several times along their journeys. They were flying in a plane with literally no instruments—not even a radio—and they had road maps instead of aerial maps, and some of those weren't even correct. My grandfather had this desire for adventure, exploration, doing crazy things."[2] Somewhere along the way, old Joshua Haldeman, his grandfather, became a model, a person that was worth his admiration.

In her youth, Maye was a nerd who liked science and did well in her coursework. She and Errol grew up in the same neighborhood, and he was taken with her good looks. He courted her for seven years before she finally accepted to marry him. Their marriage was never a happy one. Elon was a curious and energetic toddler, and just like any mother would, Maye thought of him as being special and smarter than the other kids.

---

[2] Ashlee Vance (2015), "Elon Musk: Tesla, SpaceX, and the Quest for a Fantastic Future," pages 20–21.

He spent most of his early childhood with his sister Tosca and his brother Kimbal to whom he was the closest, and they were frequently watched by a housekeeper as their parents spent a lot of time away. In 1980, his parents went through a divorce. Maye took the kids and moved in Durban, on the eastern coast of South Africa. After a while, Elon decided to live with his father. "My father seemed sort of sad and lonely, and my mom had three kids, and he didn't have any. It seemed unfair," Musk recalled.[3] This decision was a hard one on Maye, who felt betrayed, but she respected his decision. Soon, Kimbal joined him as he believed that a son should be with his father.

Musk remembers about his father that he was not very talkative. "He would just drink whiskey and be grumpy and was very good at doing crossword puzzles."[4] Rather than bonding with his father, it was his grandmother, or Nana as the brother called her, who influenced both his and Kimbal's life. "After the divorce, she took care of me quite a lot. She would pick me up from school, and I would hang out with her, playing Scrabble and that type of thing," Musk said while Kimbal remembers her as a "dominant and enterprising woman."[5] Errol had a big house, with plenty of money that allowed the kids to experience numerous luxuries, such as books, computers, and trips overseas. He also made sure that the kids' minds stay sharp by dealing out practical lessons, such as taking them on the sites of his engineering jobs.

Despite having privileges, living with Errol took an emotional and mental toll on the kids. Both Elon and Kimbal admitted that their childhood had fun memories but overall was harsh. "It would certainly be accurate to say that I did not have a good childhood. It may sound good. It was not absent of good, but it was not a happy childhood. It was like misery. He's good at making life miserable—that's for sure. He can take any situation no matter how good it is and make it bad. He's not a happy man. I don't know . . . fu*k . . . I don't know how someone becomes like

---

[3] Ashlee Vance (2015), "Elon Musk: Tesla, SpaceX, and the Quest for a Fantastic Future," page 23.

[4] Ashlee Vance (2015), "Elon Musk: Tesla, SpaceX, and the Quest for a Fantastic Future," page 23.

[5] Ashlee Vance (2015), "Elon Musk: Tesla, SpaceX, and the Quest for a Fantastic Future," page 23.

he is. It would just cause too much trouble to tell you anymore," Musk explained to Ashlee Vance.[6]

Looking back, Musk now considers that to have been a mistake, calling his father an "odd duck" and "a terrible human being." Errol remarried and had two daughters that the Musk family is very fond of. It is widely believed that the Musk's made the conscious choice of not bad-mouthing Errol in public as to protect the girls. As an adult, though, he has severed all ties with his parents. As of this day, Errol never met his grandkids.

In an email to Ashlee Vance, Errol described his son and his feelings toward him: "Elon was a very independent and focused child at home with me. He loved computer science before anyone even knew what it was in South Africa and his ability was widely recognized by the time he was 12 years old. Elon and his brother Kimbal's activities as children and young men were so many and varied that it's difficult to name just one, as they traveled together with me extensively in S. Africa and the world at large, visiting all the continents regularly from the age of six onwards. Elon and his brother and sister were and continue to be exemplary, in every way a father could want. I'm very proud of what Elon's accomplished."[7]

Elon was a peculiar kid from the very start, his introspectiveness going as far as pushing people to believe that he was deaf. His pensiveness was so intense that his brothers could yell or cause a ruckus beside him without him noticing. Maye said about his nature, "Well, it didn't change . . . He goes into his brain, and then you just see he is in another world. He still does that. Now I just leave him be because I know he is designing a new rocket or something."[8]

Musk's way of describing his "episodes" is rather interesting. He claims that as a child, he could see images in his mind, clear and detailed, much like a drawing made by computer software. He recounts them as follows: "It seems as though the part of the brain that's usually reserved

---

[6] Ashlee Vance (2015), "Elon Musk: Tesla, SpaceX, and the Quest for a Fantastic Future," page 24.

[7] Ashlee Vance (2015), "Elon Musk: Tesla, SpaceX, and the Quest for a Fantastic Future," page 24.

[8] Ashlee Vance (2015), "Elon Musk: Tesla, SpaceX, and the Quest for a Fantastic Future," page 21.

for visual processing—the part that is used to process images coming in from my eyes—gets taken over by internal thought processes. I can't do this as much now because there are so many things demanding my attention, but as a kid, it happened a lot. That large part of your brain that's used to handle incoming images gets used for internal thinking."[9]

He was also an avid reader, books being there for him to entertain and fuel his future ambitions. His where comics, nonfiction books, and a good deal of science fiction novels, in which he's completely get lost for hours. Some of the titles that marked him are Tolkien's *The Lord of the Rings* and Douglas Adams's *The Hitchhiker's Guide to the Galaxy*. However, it was Isaac Asimov's Foundation series that told him a lesson that would greatly influence him: "You should try to take the set of actions that are likely to prolong civilization, minimize the probability of a dark age, and reduce the length of a dark age if there is one."[10] He was so involved in his reading that, there was a moment when there was nothing else to read. He said, "At one point, I ran out of books to read at the school library and the neighborhood library. This is maybe the third or fourth grade. I tried to convince the librarian to order books for me. So then, I started to read the *Encyclopedia Britannica*. That was so helpful. You don't know what you don't know. You realize there are all these things out there."[11]

This reading spree was a sort of existential crisis for the young Musk. Where religious and philosophical texts failed, sci-fi and comics prevailed. It's comics that told him to "try and save the world." For him, comics made it seem like "one should try to make the world a better place because the inverse makes no sense." Sci-fi gems made him understand that what matters most is the type of questions to ask. Then, "Once you figure out the question, then the answer is relatively easy. I came to the conclusion that really we should aspire to increase the scope and scale of human consciousness in order to better understand what questions to ask."[12] It all culminated in an ultimate life statement

---

[9] Ashlee Vance (2015), "Elon Musk: Tesla, SpaceX, and the Quest for a Fantastic Future," page 22.

[10] Strauss Neil (2017), "Elon Musk: The Architect of Tomorrow," *Rolling Stone.*

[11] Ashlee Vance (2015), "Elon Musk: Tesla, SpaceX, and the Quest for a Fantastic Future," page 22.

[12] Ashlee Vance (2015), "Elon Musk: Tesla, SpaceX, and the Quest for a Fantastic Future," page 18.

that Musk has fully adopted, "To strive for the greater collective enlightenment," the fate of man in the universe becoming his personal obligation. Saying that Elon Musk liked books as a child is a major understatement. Books shaped his way of thinking and gave his life a purpose. Musk said, "I was raised by books. Books, and then my parents."

Because the boy had a memory to die for, which was photographic, all his intensive reading turned him into a know-it-all sort of kid. Maye recalled, "If we had a question, Tosca would always say, 'Just ask genius boy.' We could ask him about anything. He just remembered it." Musk was a bookworm and a geek. And he also had a liking to correct people, although not out of malice but for the sake of telling them what was factually right. It's fair to say that normal kids don't take too much to such behaviors, so more often than not, he was the odd one out. Maye remembered, "They would say, 'Elon, we are not playing with you anymore.' I felt very sad as a mother because I think he wanted friends. Kimbal and Tosca would bring home friends, and Elon wouldn't, and he would want to play with them. But he was awkward, you know."[13] Even his siblings were not very attached to him in these early stages of their childhood, but as they grew, their relationship became stronger and more affectionate. He became their leader when it came to mischief.

But Elon's nerdiness ran deeper than being an outcast or a bookworm. While his parents were away, he would engage himself in dangerous experiments involving explosives and rocket building, a foreshadowing of his future in engineering. He would just create his own compounds, and to his surprise, they would really explode. "Saltpeter, sulfur, and charcoal are the basic ingredients for gunpowder, and then if you combine a strong acid with a strong alkaline, that will generally release a lot of energy. Granulated chlorine with brake fluid—that's quite impressive," he later explained his endeavors.[14] Although looking back on those days, he admitted that his trials were on the dangerous side and that he's "shocked" to have kept all his fingers. He was also a Dungeons & Dragons master, adoring the role-playing fantasy game to the core, and his outstanding imagination captivated his teammates.

---

[13] Ashlee Vance (2015), "Elon Musk: Tesla, SpaceX, and the Quest for a Fantastic Future," page 23.

[14] Ashlee Vance (2015), "Elon Musk: Tesla, SpaceX, and the Quest for a Fantastic Future," page 25.

His businessman flair was as well present since his early years. He, along with his brother and cousins, had a whole Easter egg sale business going for them. The kids would travel to the wealthier parts of the South African capital, and they would sell the sweet treats for $10 apiece, which was roughly twenty times the cost of making them. The price was clearly on the stiff side, but the clever entrepreneurs knew that the people could afford them and had no other means of buying the chocolate scams.

At the age of ten, he developed a liking for computing with the Commodore VIC-20, an 8-bit home computer that was very popular at that time, and he "hounded" his father to buy it for him. He was so hooked that he taught himself computer programming, as his first computer came with a workbook on basic programming. He said, "It was supposed to take like six months to get through all the lessons. I just got super OCD on it and stayed up for three days with no sleep and did the entire thing. It seemed like the most super-compelling thing I had ever seen."[15]

At the age of twelve, he created Blastar, a science-fiction-style game that was similar to the arcade classic Space Invaders. A brief description of the game states, "In this game, you have to destroy an alien space freighter, which is carrying deadly Hydrogen Bombs and Status Beam Machines. This game makes good use of sprites and animation, and in this sense makes the listing worth reading."[16] Even if Musk himself found it to be ordinary, the young Elon sold the code of the game to the *PC and Office Technology* magazine, a transaction which earned him $500. A web version of the game is still available today.

Not all was rosy for young Musk. He was severely bullied through his childhood because of his stature and nerdy interests, as well as for his unusual name and his privileged status. The bullies went as far as forming gangs to "hunt him down," doing horrible things like pushing him down the stairs or brutally beating him. "I was almost beaten to death," Musk would say later on a *60 Minutes* interview. Besides being hospitalized, he also had to undergo a "nose job" in order to fix some of

---

[15] Ashlee Vance (2015), "Elon Musk: Tesla, SpaceX, and the Quest for a Fantastic Future," page 25.

[16] Elon Musk (1984), "Blastar," *PC and Office Technology.*

the damages. Musk never knew why he was the ultimate target. "For some reason, they decided that I was it, and they were going to go after me nonstop. That's what made growing up difficult. For a number of years, there was no respite. You get chased around by gangs at school who tried to beat the shit out of me, and then I'd come home, and it would just be awful there as well. It was just like nonstop horrible," he confessed.[17]

The bullying stopped when he went to a growth spurt and dedicated some of his time to learn how to defend himself. His karate, wrestling, and judo classes paid off, with him being able to get back to the attackers "as hard as they gave it to him."

All throughout his childhood, Musk was aware of the dangers that defied living in South Africa. It could be violent and brutal, especially for some kids. Even so, Musk and his brother Kimbal would often take the ominous trip from Pretoria to Johannesburg, a feat that put a mark on their personalities and views. Kimbal would later say regarding his childhood, "South Africa was not a happy-go-lucky place, and that has an impact on you. We saw some really rough stuff. It was part of an atypical upbringing—just this insane set of experiences that changes how you view risk. You don't grow up thinking getting a job is the hard part. That's not interesting enough."[18]

Education

In South Africa

Elon Musk attended a private primary school, Waterkloof House Preparatory School, and a public coed high school called Bryanston, where he spent the eighth and ninth grades. Ultimately, he graduated from Pretoria Boys High School, a public institution that charged for tuition.

Although public, Pretoria High functioned more like a private institution, and it was known as the sort of place to send a young person if you

---

[17] Ashlee Vance (2015), "Elon Musk: Tesla, SpaceX, and the Quest for a Fantastic Future," page 26.
[18] Ashlee Vance (2015), "Elon Musk: Tesla, SpaceX, and the Quest for a Fantastic Future," page 25.

want a bright academic future for them. Musk did not stand out as one of the brightest kids, and his lack of interest in sports did not make him popular. Most of his old classmates claim that there were no signs for what Musk was going to become. But what some do remember is his interest in the importance of solar power and rockets—he would occasionally bring models to school. He would talk about colonizing other planets and whether people would ever switch to "paperless banking." It's fair to say that in his high school years, he already had his main interests figured out. He was chosen for an experimental computer program in which he had the chance to learn three programming languages: BASIC, COBOL, and Pascal. These things would come in handy later on.

According to Musk, not excelling in school was a personal choice. "I just look at it as 'What grades do I need to get where I want to go?' There were compulsory subjects like Afrikaans, and I just didn't see the point of learning that. It seemed ridiculous. I'd get a passing grade and that was fine. Things like physics and computers—I got the highest grade you can get in those. There needs to be a reason for a grade. I'd rather play video games, write software, and read books than try and get an A if there's no point in getting an A. I can remember failing subjects in like fourth and fifth grade. Then, my mother's boyfriend told me I'd be held back if I didn't pass. I didn't actually know you had to pass the subjects to move to the next grade. I got the best grades in class after that," he explained his reasoning.[19]

Musk went against his father's wishes to attend a college in Pretoria and instead focused his goal on getting to the United States because he believed that "America is where great things are possible, more than any other country in the world." He did attend the University of Pretoria for a few months before going on with his dream. According to him, his experience at the university was just a way to fill up the time while he waited for his Canadian papers. It took one year for Musk to get his documentation.

---

[19] Ashlee Vance (2015), "Elon Musk: Tesla, SpaceX, and the Quest for a Fantastic Future," page 27.

In Canada

He obtained a Canadian passport through his mother after an unexpected change of law that allowed Maye to pass down her citizenship to her children, and he moved to Canada in June 1989, being aware that the transition to the United States would be easier that way. The move also allowed him to avoid mandatory military service in the South African military as he was just about to turn eighteen years old. He arrived in North America with "$2,000, a backpack, and a suitcase full of books," he stated on his Twitter account.

Musk had planned to live with a great-uncle in Montreal, but as chance has it, the uncle had gone to Minnesota and the young man was left with few choices. He stayed at a hostel for a few days in which he explored the city, then he headed out to a cousin. The next year of Musk's life was spent on the run through Canada, meeting family members and doing odd jobs like tending vegetables, cutting logs with a chainsaw, and cleaning the boiler room of a lumber mill. The last one he reckoned as being the hardest: "You have to put on this hazmat suit and then shimmy through this little tunnel that you can barely fit in. Then you have a shovel and you take the sand and goop and other residue, which is still steaming hot, and you have to shovel it through the same hole you came through. There is no escape. Someone else on the other side has to shovel it into a wheelbarrow. If you stay in there for more than thirty minutes, you get too hot and die."[20] His brother would soon reunite with him, and together, they matured in Canada.

Musk attended Queen's University, and in 1992, he left to study physics and business at the University of Pennsylvania. He got an undergraduate degree in economics and stayed for a second degree in physics, his other passion.

His reason for choosing Queens was as youthful as it could be: there were more good-looking women at Queens. Other than studies, Elon and Kimbal had a weird habit of going through newspapers and finding people that they would like to meet. Businesspeople, writers, no one

---

[20] Ashlee Vance (2015), "Elon Musk: Tesla, SpaceX, and the Quest for a Fantastic Future," page 29.

could escape the obnoxious and never-ending phone calls of the Musk brothers, who inquired if they wanted to have lunch with them. Peter Nicholson, the top executive at the Bank of Nova Scotia was one of the few "victims" that agreed. He told Ashlee Vance, "I was not in the habit of getting out-of-the-blue requests. I was perfectly prepared to have lunch with a couple of kids that had that kind of gumption." The meeting was an interesting one for Nicholson: "I became more impressed and fascinated as I talked to them. They were so determined." By the end of the lunch, he was so impressed that he offered Elon a summer internship at the bank.

Christie, a science writer and Nicholson's daughter, had the chance to meet the boys at Elon's birthday party. She remembers that Elon was nice and polite to her, but considering that they were meeting for the first time, he had no qualms to start off a conversation on a peculiar topic. "I believe the second sentence out of his mouth was 'I think a lot about electric cars,'" Christie said. "And then he turned to me and said, 'Do you think about electric cars?'" This question baffled her and forever branded that moment in her memory. According to her, she could tell that he was "different," and that made him captivating. They went on to become good friends, and they would often engage in deep conversations on the phone. "One night, he told me, 'If there was a way that I could not eat so I could work more, I would not eat. I wish there was a way to get nutrients without sitting down for a meal.' The enormity of his work ethic at that age and his intensity jumped out. It seemed like one of the more unusual things I had ever heard," she recalled one that left her thinking.[21]

During his time at Queens, he met Navaid Farooq, who happened to be his roommate. They got along very well, with Musk calling him "a great guy" and being thankful for the fact that he attended all the lectures and let Elon borrow his notes. Musk himself went to "the least number of classes possible" and spent his time selling computer parts or PC built by him to make some extra money. He would "build something to suit their needs like a tricked-out gaming machine or a simple word processor that cost less than what they could get in a store,"

[21] Ashlee Vance (2015), "Elon Musk: Tesla, SpaceX, and the Quest for a Fantastic Future," page 30.

Musk said. "Or if their computer didn't boot properly or had a virus, I'd fix it. I could pretty much solve any problem."[22] Although not very keen on going to courses, in his college years, Musk stood out more than in high school by attending public-speaking competitions and displaying some characters traits that defy him today, like stubbornness and his intensity regarding his goals. When asked about Musk, Farooq described him as follows: "When Elon gets into something, he develops just this different level of interest in it than other people. That is what differentiates Elon from the rest of humanity." The two remained good friends.

Queens was a great experience for the young Elon Musk, but at the University of Pennsylvania, he found something new: people that thought like him. Maye reminisced back to those times: "There were some nerds there. He so enjoyed them. I remember going for lunch with them, and they were talking physics things. They were saying, 'A plus B equals pi squared' or whatever. They would laugh out loud. It was cool to see him so happy."[23]

At Penn, he met Adeo Ressi, one of Elon's lifelong friends. During the week, they would study together, but come the weekend and their place became a certified nightclub. Ressi was the one that knew how to build up the atmosphere, decorating the words with bright colors and weird objects, putting garbage bags on the windows to make the room darker and so on. They charged five dollars for entry, and they offered the whole package with drinks and whatever they would need. Their success was greater than expected, and they could gather up as many as five hundred people in a day of "activity." Ressi was a very free spirit regarding his art, and one time, he went as far as nailing Elon's desk to a wall and painting it in glowing colors. Musk retaliated by getting his desk down.

Elon was not the party kind of guy. He did not drink, but he made sure that everything was in check: "I was paying my own way through college and could make an entire month's rent in one night. Adeo was in

---

[22] Ashlee Vance (2015), "Elon Musk: Tesla, SpaceX, and the Quest for a Fantastic Future," page 31.

[23] Ashlee Vance (2015), "Elon Musk: Tesla, SpaceX, and the Quest for a Fantastic Future," page 32.

charge of doing cool shit around the house, and I would run the party."[24] For him, the parties were a means to an end, not a source of entertainment. Ressi talked about Elon's behavior during the parties: "Elon was the most straight-laced dude you have ever met. He never drank. He never did anything. Zero. Literally nothing."[25]

Also at Penn, he went further on with his interests by writing three innovative papers.

1. "The Importance of Being Solar"—the material predicted how solar power will rise and how solar cells would function, along with a drawing for the "power station of the future." He received a 98 mark on it.

2. About electronically scanning books and documents and putting them into a database.

3. Ultracapacitors—one of his favorite subject, as he found them to be potential energy storage for his future ventures. He got a 97 mark and the teacher's praises.

To the latter, he mentioned the result from a Silicon Valley research: "The end result represents the first new means of storing significant amounts of electrical energy since the development of the battery and fuel cell. Furthermore, because the Ultra capacitor retains the basic properties of a capacitor, it can deliver its energy over one hundred times faster than a battery of equivalent weight, and be recharged just as quickly." Saying that he was excited about ultra-capacitors might be an understatement, but what the teacher was most surprised of was Musk's ability to take physics concepts and put them in actual business plans, a trait that helped Elon Musk succeed in all his ventures.

In that span of time, Musk began to seriously consider his future. He was a total video game nerd, so the thought of getting into the business came to his mind more than once. "I really like computer games, but then if I made really great computer games, how much effect would that have on the world. It wouldn't have a big effect. Even though I

---

[24] Ashlee Vance (2015), "Elon Musk: Tesla, SpaceX, and the Quest for a Fantastic Future," page 32.
[25] Ashlee Vance (2015), "Elon Musk: Tesla, SpaceX, and the Quest for a Fantastic Future," page 32.

have an intrinsic love of video games, I couldn't bring myself to do that as a career."[26] His childhood motivation for doing something big, something that would "save the word" was greater than his love for video games.

While other future Silicon Valley entrepreneurs "sniffed out trends," Musk was identifying the areas that would change the most in the coming years: renewable energy, space, and the internet. He decided then that he would leave his mark on them all, and he shared that with anyone that was willing to listen—mostly his ex-girlfriends and, ultimately, his ex-wives. Skeptics don't really buy into this "master plan" idea, that Musk knew from the very beginning what he was going to do, but according to him, "I really was thinking about this stuff in college. It is not some invented story after the fact. I don't want to seem like a Johnny-come-lately or that I'm chasing a fad or just being opportunistic. I'm not an investor. I like to make technologies real that I think are important for the future and useful in some sort of way."[27]

He paid his own expenses through college life, with his nightclub gig and whatever money he managed to make out of PC sales.

Elon wanted to further his studies in energy physics with a PhD at Stanford University, but this moment in his life coincided with the internet boom and the economic bubble, which oversaw an extreme growth in the usage and potential of the internet. After only two days at Stanford, an ambitious Musk dropped out in order to be part of the new economic era by launching his first company, Zip2 Corporation, despite having a $110k college debt.

Elon Musk is not the type of guy that looks down on others regarding their educational status. In 2018, when a Harvard graduate bragged about how "you can't succeed in life without a degree" and implying a sense of superiority over his schooling pedigree, Musk promptly replied to his arrogant tweet. He pointed out that schooling should not be confused with education, and while he himself did not attend the prestigious university, some people that worked for him did.

---

[26] Ashlee Vance (2015), "Elon Musk: Tesla, SpaceX, and the Quest for a Fantastic Future," page 33.
[27] Ashlee Vance (2015), "Elon Musk: Tesla, SpaceX, and the Quest for a Fantastic Future," page 33.

Chapter 2: Zip2 Corporation

Before Zip2

In the summer of 1994, Musk was mostly in Silicon Valley, holding down some internships. During the day, he worked at Pinnacle Research Institute, which was a start-up where researchers studied ultra-capacitors and their potential of being used as fuels. Musk already had a deep interest in ultra-capacitors, and he enjoyed his work at Pinnacle and even used it as inspiration for his papers at Penn.

In evenings, Musk worked at the Rocket Science Games (another start-up but, this time, a video-games-focused one), which had the ambition of moving games from cartridges to CDs—adding production quality to the games. He had a very easy coding job there, which required him to write drivers that would allow mice and joysticks to work with different computers and for different games. But he did not like this easy task, so he went on to do his own thing. "I was basically trying to figure out how you could multitask stuff so you could read video from a CD while running a game at the same time. At the time, you could do one or the other. It was this complicated bit of assembly programming," he explained his endeavors.[28] He was stubborn and "unflappable," so the people at Rocket Science Games just let him do whatever he wanted.

When the call of the internet became irresistible, both Musk brothers moved together to start on their Web journey. His first business idea came to Musk while attending to his internships. A salesperson for the Yellow Pages came one day and tried to sell his idea of listing companies online, but he sold his idea very poorly. Elon, however, saw the potential, and he told Kimbal about a business in which they could help companies go online. "Elon said, 'These guys don't know what they are

---

[28] Ashlee Vance (2015), "Elon Musk: Tesla, SpaceX, and the Quest for a Fantastic Future," page 37.

talking about. Maybe this is something we can do,'" Kimbal remembered a part of their conversation.

The Company

Zip2, or the Global Link Information Network, was a company that provided local businesses with an internet presence as well as assisting newspapers in creating and licensing online city guides.

It was founded in 1995 by Musk, his brother, and Greg Kouri after Musk acquired a disc that contained a business directory and managed to persuade Navteq, an electronic navigation maps provider, to offer him a mapping software for free. He created a code that merged the two separate databases together—maps and businesses—and reasoned that anyone should be able to find the closest pizza place and have a way of getting there. Initially, investors were hard to come by and Musk & Co. lived in their office in order to keep expenses at a minimum. Musk later remarked how hard those times were for him and his brother. Besides sleeping on couches, they "showered at the YMCA," and they had it so rough that they only had one computer. He worked relentlessly, seven days a week, spending all nights coding so the site could be up during the day.

In a Twitter post, he recollected the type of work that he did at Zip2: "I wrote entire V1 of software for drawing vector maps and calculating point to point directions anywhere in the US (first ever company to do so), as well as white pages and business listings with reviews (an early Yelp). Also wrote V1 of classifieds, auto trading, and real estate apps."

The two brothers started making hires, and they managed to assemble a sales team, which included Jeff Heilman and Craig Mohr. They went with the door-to-door sales strategy, and things were going slow. When Mohr decided to start "courting" auto dealerships, nobody had any expectations. But Mohr delivered. "One day I came back with about nine hundred dollars in checks. I walked into the office and asked the guys what they wanted me to do with the money. Elon stopped pounding his keyboard, leaned out from behind his monitor, and said, 'No way, you've got money.'"[29] Mohr recalled that glorious moment.

---

[29] Ashlee Vance (2015), "Elon Musk: Tesla, SpaceX, and the Quest for a Fantastic Future," page 39.

Their service was not perfect. It would often fail to load or load exorbitantly slow, but the Musk brothers knew how to make their product appealing to future investors. In order to impress them, they created a big case and put it on their PC and added the whole ordeal to a wheeled base. When by chance investors were at the door they would show off their massive "machine," and some would fall for the gimmick. "Even then, as essentially a college kid with zits, Elon had this drive that this thing—whatever it was—had to get done and that if he didn't do it, he'd miss his shot. I think that's what the VCs saw—that he was willing to stake his existence on building out this platform," Heilman told Ashlee Vance.[30]

The money needed for setting up the company mostly came from angel investors, but Kouri himself came in with US$6,000, which he gave right off the bat when the boys announced they were moving the business to California, and in 1996 he followed them. They also coerced businesses to pay for their inclusion in order to expand its listing. Founded in Palo Alto, California, the company focused on helping local businesses by providing guidance and linking their services to those that searched for them.

Kouri was the adult at Zip2, and he came with an experience that was much needed, serving soon as a mentor for the young Musk. Derek Proudian, the chief executive officer of Zip2, described the relationship between Kouri and Musk: "Really smart people sometimes don't understand that not everyone can keep up with them or go as fast. Greg is one of the few people that Elon would listen to and had a way of putting things in context for him."[31] Kouri also acted as a referee in Elon and Kimbal's fights, which were actual fist fights. The brothers would fight anytime they did not agree on something as both had very strict visions and had a hard time accepting anyone else's ideas but their own. They stopped the "fight club" only when they went over the top and Kouri put a definite end to the squabbling.

Kouri would go on to invest in Musk's future ventures, and Musk attended his funeral in 2012. Both he and Kimbal have only kind words to

---

[30] Ashlee Vance (2015), "Elon Musk: Tesla, SpaceX, and the Quest for a Fantastic Future," page 39.

[31] Ashlee Vance (2015), "Elon Musk: Tesla, SpaceX, and the Quest for a Fantastic Future," page 40.

say about their late mentor.

Global Link received a major US$3 million investment from Mohr Davidow Ventures in 1996, and they officially changed the name to Zip2. Mohr Davidow is a venture capital firm that focuses on start-up and early-stage investments with a big interest in Internet services. They changed Zip2's strategy from direct localized business sales to selling national back-end software packages to news outlets in order to help them build their own directories. Besides that, they gave Zip2 the chance to hire talented engineers, which the company desperately needed.

They also made Richard Sorkin CEO because he was a more experienced businessman, so the investors favored him. Musk reluctantly agreed with the change and came to regret his decision later on. Jim Ambras, the vice president of engineering, also shared Musk's remorse: "Probably the biggest regret the whole time I worked with him was that he had made a deal with the devil with Mohr Davidow."[32]

Ambras was a former employee at Silicon Graphics Inc., and he was one of the most talented engineers they had. With his connections and the promise of internet riches, Ambras managed to steal SGI's "best guys," much to Musk's delight. His delight turned to anguish fast when the new team of engineers started rewriting his software. Musk was good at coding, but he was not a professional. The new team managed to shrink down the endless lines of code and bring some structure to the software. They also generated real deadlines while Musk had a very arbitrary way of seeing and calculating how much time it would take him to get something done. Ambras explained to Ashlee Vance how Elon worked with time: "If you asked Elon how long it would take to do something, there was never anything in his mind that would take more than an hour. We came to interpret an hour as really taking a day or two, and if Elon ever did say something would take a day, we allowed for a week or two weeks."[33]

[32] Ashlee Vance (2015), "Elon Musk: Tesla, SpaceX, and the Quest for a Fantastic Future," page 41.
[33] Ashlee Vance (2015), "Elon Musk: Tesla, SpaceX, and the Quest for a Fantastic Future," page 41.

When Elon did not agree with something that the engineered did, he would just go and change it when they left as he would often be the one to work late hours, which caused some friction. He still remembers those days and what he thought at that time: "Yeah, we had some very good software engineers at Zip2, but I mean, I could code way better than them. And I'd just go in and fix their fucking code. I would be frustrated waiting for their stuff, so I'm going to go and fix your code, and now it runs five times faster, you idiot. There was one guy who wrote a quantum mechanics equation, a quantum probability on the board, and he got it wrong. I'm like, 'How can you write that?' Then I corrected it for him. He hated me after that. Eventually, I realized, okay, I might have fixed that thing, but now I've made the person unproductive. It just wasn't a good way to go about things."[34]

Obviously, Elon was not the greatest team player, but according to Justine, he tried to temper his character as best as he could in those early days of Zip2: "Elon is not someone who would say, 'I feel you. I see your point of view,' because he doesn't have that 'I feel you' dimension. There were things that seemed obvious to other people that weren't that obvious to him. He had to learn that a twenty-something-year-old shouldn't really shoot down the plans of older, senior people and point out everything wrong with them. He learned to modify his behavior in certain ways. I just think he comes at the world through strategy and intellect."[35] Even if he tried to temper himself, he still came off as abrasive to some of his employees. For him "no" was not an acceptable answer and "impossible" did not exist. He wanted things done. Being nice was not one of his concerns.

But he was good at energizing people. Whenever an investor had to arrive, he rallied the people to create a buzzing atmosphere as to show how successful the enterprise was. He created a video-game team and encouraged them to participate in competitions as a team-building exercise and a way to earn some extra bucks as they did manage to win "a few thousand dollars." Their business was starting to go well because newspapers started to realize that the internet could be a real

---

[34] Ashlee Vance (2015), "Elon Musk: Tesla, SpaceX, and the Quest for a Fantastic Future," pages 43–44.

[35] Ashlee Vance (2015), "Elon Musk: Tesla, SpaceX, and the Quest for a Fantastic Future," page 41.

threat to them. They had to either join it or be beaten by it. And they all wanted to be part of the online world.

Their product was called Auto Guide, which connected online newspaper readers with car sellers and local dealerships. It allowed for direct two-way communication between the people that needed services and advertisers. The users of Auto Guide could message the advertisers via fax machines, and advertisers could have access to the said message by using some specific URLs.

Musk was appointed the chief officer of the technology department, while Rich Sorkin, the Silicon Valley entrepreneur, played the executive role. The company continued to grow, and it trademarked its official slogan: "We Power the Press." Under Sorkin, Zip2 had struck deals with the worldwide influent *New York Times* newspaper as well as with the American media company Knight Ridder and the mass media and business conglomerate Hearst Corporation. Those collaborations made Zip2 a major part of the newspaper industry's inclusion into the online city guide industry.

The company was partnered up with about 160 newspapers to develop guides both locally and on full scales. Musk assessed that twenty of those newspapers led to full-scale city guides. According to the *New York Times*, besides their core services of guide development, Zip2 also offered an online directory, an email, and a calendar.

Musk was somewhat unhappy with how things were unraveling for Zip2. He wanted to offer services directly to consumers, not to be a behind-the-scenes tool for newspapers. But Sorkin believes that the media company was paying too well to change up the game. The consumers' path was simply not feasible enough in his perception.

In 1998, there was a merge between Zip2 and CitySearch, another online city guide developer and the company's biggest competitor. The deal was arranged by Sorkin as a means of expanding the company. Despite initially agreeing with the fusion, Musk later changed his mind and managed to persuade the directors into declining the deal. He created a revolt that as a result saw Sorkin removed from his CEO position and replaced with Derek Proudian, who was at the time a general partner with Mohr Davidow Ventures. The two companies agreed to disagree and cited "incompatibilities in cultures and technology" as a reason for the failed unification.

However, the whole merger ordeal put a strain in Sorkin and Musk's relationship. Sorkin wanted the merger to happen, and he blamed Musk's "atrocious behavior" for the failure. Proudian tried to manage the situation as well as he could: "There was a lot of backlash and finger-pointing. Elon wanted to be CEO, but I said, 'This is your first company. Let's find an acquirer and make some money, so you can do your second, third, and fourth company.'"[36]

After the deal with CitySearch was off, Zip2 found itself in a bad situation. It was losing money, and Musk still persisted in his consumer route despite Proudian telling him that they did not have the capital for it. When Compaq Computers showed interest in Zip2, it was like a blessing for the troubled company.

Ultimately, in February 1999, Compaq Computers, a company that dealt with computer developments, sales, and computer-related products and services, acquired Zip2 to enhance their AltaVista web search, one of the most used early search engines, by adding some local breath. The price paid was US$307 million, out of which Elon netted US$22 million and his brother $15 million since they were the original founders.

Elon had no interest in sticking with Zip2 after the sale, and neither did Kimbal. "We were overwhelmed and just thought these guys must know what they're doing. But they didn't. There was no vision once they took over. They were investors, and we got on well with them, but the vision had just disappeared from the company," Kimbal would later say about the sale.[37]

Regarding his time at Zip2, Musk reluctantly admitted to Ashlee Vance that he could have done a better job handling the people and the business: "I had never really run a team of any sort before. I'd never been a sports captain or a captain of anything or managed a single person. I had to think, Okay, what are the things that affect how a team func-

---

[36] Ashlee Vance (2015), "Elon Musk: Tesla, SpaceX, and the Quest for a Fantastic Future," page 43.

[37] Ashlee Vance (2015), "Elon Musk: Tesla, SpaceX, and the Quest for a Fantastic Future," page 43.

tions? The first obvious assumption would be that other people will behave like you. But that's not true. Even if they would like to behave like you, they don't necessarily have all the assumptions or information that you have in your mind. So if I know a certain set of things and I talk to a replica of myself but only communicate half the information, you can't expect that the replica would come to the same conclusion. You have to put yourself in a position where you say, 'Well, how would this sound to them, knowing what they know?'"[38]

Although it's been years since his debut in the business world with the Zip2 company, Musk still keeps some old traditions alive. He told CBS's King that he frequently sleeps at his Tesla Motors office on a couch or even on the floor because "the couch was too narrow." This confession prompted YouTuber Ben Sullins to start a GoFundMe campaign in order to deliver Musk a new couch as well as raise money for charity. Wayfair, an online furniture company, indeed donated a more suitable addition to the billionaire's office, but the whole purpose was to promote the charity campaign, which ended up raising more than $18,000, including Musk's own contribution. Many people considered this ordeal to be a publicity stunt orchestrated by Musk's team since the mogul could easily afford to buy his own couch.

But at the end of the day, a substantial amount of money went to a good cause, whether it was just a stunt or a humoristic situation that sparked interest in charity that Musk was glad to be part of.

---

[38] Ashlee Vance (2015), "Elon Musk: Tesla, SpaceX, and the Quest for a Fantastic Future," page 43.

Chapter 3: X.com and PayPal

A Dot-Com Millionaire

Musk became a millionaire in a matter of a few years, and that would be enough for someone to lose his head a little. For him, that showed by buying a McLaren F1 sports car, which was a limited edition and only the crème de la crème owned one. He made a publicized event out of the delivery of the car by inviting CNN to film it. "There are sixty-two McLarens in the world, and I will own one of them. Wow, I can't believe it's actually here. That's pretty wild, man," he said at the sight of his new ride.

Despite that, he was not the kind to keep it for special occasions. He would drive it around the city, park it in a parking lot of a Safeway, and he even tried to contact other owners for races. That car that some called "a work of art" ended up being totaled by Musk, who found it very funny that the car "was not even insured."

While he did dabble in some eccentricities, he never lost sight of his goal. He wanted to start another business, right when Zip2 was slowly sinking down into the Compaq label. His inspiration came from his internship at the Bank Nova Scotia. He happened to observe an opportunity where no one else did: "I calculated the backstop value, and it was something like fifty cents on the dollar, while the actual debt was trading at twenty-five cents. This was like the biggest opportunity ever, and nobody seemed to realize it."[39] For a second opinion, he called Goldman Sachs, a big trader in the market. When Musk was asked how much would he want, he allegedly "came up with some ridiculous number like ten billion dollars," and his jaw dropped when Sachs told him it was doable, because the United States tried to help reduce the debt for

---

[39] Ashlee Vance (2015), "Elon Musk: Tesla, SpaceX, and the Quest for a Fantastic Future," page 46.

countries like Brazil and Argentina. The whole business was backed up by Uncle Sam. Basically, he could double his money and lose nothing.

He tried to pitch his idea to his boss, but the bank did not want to be "burned" again on South American countries' debt. Musk told Ashlee Vance his thoughts on the matter: "I tried to tell them that's not the point. The point is that it's fucking backed by Uncle Sam. It doesn't matter what the South Americans do. You cannot lose unless you think the US Treasury is going to default. But they still didn't do it, and I was stunned. Later in life, as I competed against the banks, I would think back to this moment, and it gave me confidence. All the bankers did was copy what everyone else did. If everyone else ran off a bloody cliff, they'd run right off a cliff with them. If there was a giant pile of gold sitting in the middle of the room and nobody was picking it up, they wouldn't pick it up, either."[40]

The idea of starting an internet bank flourished in his mind, an idea that he shared with his fellows at Pinnacle Research. He really believed that the finance industry needed to change and that he could have a big influence on banking if given the chance. There were some setbacks to his plan. At that time, people were new to the idea of the internet, and they did not trust it much. Musk wanted to build a whole financial institution online, a place where you could open checking accounts and savings, insurance, and brokerage services. The complete package. This meant a complete storm of regulations that had to be met.

When Zip2 was at its end, Musk was already formalizing his banking plan. X.com was created to make that big change he wished for.

X.com in Action

After the sale of Zip2, Musk had $22 million on hand and a desire to start something that would change a whole industry. "I could go and buy one of the islands in the Bahamas and turn it into my personal fiefdom, but I am much more interested in trying to build and create a new company," he told CNN in that interview when he received his race car, and he kept his word.

---

[40] Ashlee Vance (2015), "Elon Musk: Tesla, SpaceX, and the Quest for a Fantastic Future," pages 46–47.

That's how the idea of X.com, one of the first online banks, was born in his mind. He managed to make up a team that included Harris Fricker, Ed Ho (a former Zip2 executive), and Christopher Payne, who was Fricker's friend. Powerful names to turn his dream into an actual company.

Musk invested $12 million in the business so he can be considered the primary founder and the majority shareholder. This was a great risk for him because if things didn't work out he'd lose a whole fortune. Ho praised Musk for his eagerness to give it his all despite the situation: "That's part of what separates Elon from mere mortals. He's willing to take an insane amount of personal risk. When you do a deal like that, it either pays off or you end up in a bus shelter somewhere."[41]

X.com was the starting point of Musk's well-known style: getting into complex businesses that he had very little idea of their industries. He went on a whim that bankers were not apprehending finance efficiently, and he was confident that he could find a better alternative. All the founders agreed that the banking system needed an upgrade. In spite of their initial excitement, they soon found out that putting their plans into action would be hard. Harder than expected. Regulatory issues were atrocious.

There was a lot of pressure on the men, and they all wanted different things. Fricker wanted X.com to be run in a conventional way and had little respect for Musk's big dream of change. "We were out promising the sun, moon, and the stars to the media. Elon would say that this is not a normal business environment, and you have to suspend normal business thinking," Fricker summarized the situation.[42]

But the dream team was not meant to last. After merely five months, vision differences started showing, and spirits got heated. Ho, Fricker, and other employers left Musk on shaky grounds, with a small fraction of a workforce. This was all a result of the squabble between Fricker and Musk. It was Fricker's coup and revenge. "He said either he takes over as CEO or he's just going to take everyone from the company and

[41] Ashlee Vance (2015), "Elon Musk: Tesla, SpaceX, and the Quest for a Fantastic Future," page 48.

[42] Ashlee Vance (2015), "Elon Musk: Tesla, SpaceX, and the Quest for a Fantastic Future," page 49.

create his own company. I don't do well with blackmail. I said, 'You should go do that.' So he did," Musk told Ashlee Vance.[43]

However, young Elon was not the kind to back down. Julie Ankenbrandt, who was an early employee, can still vividly recall those times: "After all that went down, I remember sitting with Elon in his office. There were a million laws in place to block something like X.com from happening, but Elon didn't care. He just looked at me and said, 'I guess we should hire some more people.'"[44] Mike Moritz, an investor from Sequoia Capital, backed the business, while Musk was trying his best to attract engineers to his company.

He intensified his effort to raise capital and hire people, and eventually, in 1999 X.com went live. They offered a lot of features that were completely new back in the day, along with an insane $20 cash card that people would get for signing the service and a $10 cash card for every referred person.

More employees arrived at X.com, and the company managed to secure a baking license and a mutual fund license. X.com struck a partnership with the bank Barclays, and it soon created the first online bank that had insurance to back up the accounts and mutual funds for the investors.

As things usually go, others went for the same idea, and the field became competitive. X.com's biggest rival was Confinity. From the very beginning, Elon's intention for X.com was to make it a full-service online financial services firm, while Peter Thiel's start-up Confinity started on the premise to send money between Palm Pilots. Toward the end of 1999, both firms launched person-to-person payments, and Confinity's service was called PayPal. The fight between the two rivals was very intense, the two trying to outsmart each other by sweetening their promotions and widening their feature range. Confinity even went as far as offering the same signing and referring bonus system as its rival.

The fight went on, but at some point, Confinity started running out of cash. In March 2000, the two companies decided to unify since X.com

---

[43] Ashlee Vance (2015), "Elon Musk: Tesla, SpaceX, and the Quest for a Fantastic Future," page 49.

[44] Ashlee Vance (2015), "Elon Musk: Tesla, SpaceX, and the Quest for a Fantastic Future," page 49.

had the capital that Confinity lacked. Because money does the talking, the merged firm retained the name of X.com, and Elon Musk became the official CEO.

Even if they tried hard, the two teams never got along. Musk favored the product offered by X.com while everybody else put their money on PayPal. Fights broke out even when it came to the company's infrastructure. Confinity favored Linux, as it was an open-source software, while Musk preferred Microsoft's data-center software.

What started as a good business move slowly became something that would come back to bite Musk. X.com's user base grew to such a rate that its systems could not keep up. The company's website collapsed on a weekly basis. Operational inefficiencies started to pop up continuously, and to make matters worse, allegations of fraud started to emerge. X.com was "losing money hand over fist," and soon enough, the people started doubting Elon's decisions and abilities as a leader. In the eyes of the employers and his partners, Musk was not fit to be a CEO.

One night, a small group of employees gathered at a bar in Palo Alto to talk about ways of pushing Musk out. They settled on convincing the board that Thiel would come back as a CEO, but they also chose to not talk to Musk about this. They would go at it behind his back. And they did.

As soon as Musk got on the plane for his honeymoon trip, more of a fund-raising trip that would eventually end up with a stop in Sydney so they could catch the Olympics, with his then-wife Justine Musk, the wheels started spinning. In September 2000, when his plane landed, he was already denoted as CEO and replaced by Peter Thiel. He called Julie Ankerbrandt that day to find out how bad the situation was, and she, being unaware of the forces that were against him, said that "it's going to be okay." Musk went back and tried to hold his case in front of the board, but it was too late. The matter was already set in stone.

"I talked to Moritz and a few others. It wasn't so much that I wanted to be CEO but more like, 'Hey, I think there are some pretty important things that need to happen, and if I'm not CEO, I'm not sure they are going to happen.' But then I talked to Max and Peter, and it seemed like they would make these things happen. So then, I mean, it's not the end of the world."[45] Musk told Ashlee Vance about his endeavor of trying to get his company back.

Despite the nasty way he was treated, Musk stood by the company as an advisor. Still, as time went by, his influence started to drop, and X.-com was renamed PayPal after Confinity's product. Even then, he stayed as an investor and advisor. They went against his wishes to "not sell out too soon," and in 2002, PayPal was bought by eBay for $1.5 billion out of which Musk got $180 million. When the whole ordeal was done, Musk moved on by focusing on some of his more known projects.

Regarding X.com, opinions are contradictory. Many believe that Musk's outing was unfair while others agree that under him as a CEO the company would have been lost in its war against fraud. The media, however, turned on him. Eric Jackson wrote the book *The PayPal Wars: Battles with eBay, the Media, the Mafia, and the Rest of Planet Earth*, which painted Musk in the worst colors. He portrayed him as always making bad decisions and being an overall jerk while Peter Thiel was the genius that kept it all together. Valleywag, a gossip site, also jumped on the hate wagon. The critic was so outrageous that it started questioning whether or not Musk can be called a co-founder for PayPal.

That book affected Musk enough to write a lengthy email to Valleywag in 2007, presenting his side of the story. According to Musk, Jackson was much like an intern who had no idea of what was really going on backstage. He also happened to be a loyal Confinity employee, so he adored Thiel more than anything while despising Musk for his guts. Musk also pinpointed the main reasons why he can't be ruled out of the PayPal gig: he was its largest shareholder, the one that came up with the most business ideas, the one that hired talented people and the expansion that the company went through in his time as CEO.

Musk is the kind to fight when such injustice happens. According to Vince Sollitto, the former communications chief at PayPal, Musk

---

[45] Ashlee Vance (2015), "Elon Musk: Tesla, SpaceX, and the Quest for a Fantastic Future," page 52.

"comes from the school of thought in the public relations world that you let no inaccuracy go uncorrected. It sets a precedent, and you should fight every out-of-place comma tooth and nail. He takes things very personally and usually seeks war."[46] In the years to come, Musk would show the same determination wherever he wants to make a matter clear.

Nevertheless, his role in the evolution and formation of PayPal can't be ignored. He built a company out of nothing and came up with ideas that have left a mark on the payment system that we have today.

On July 5, 2017, Musk announced that he repurchased the domain name X.com from PayPal because it had "great sentimental value" to him. Later that month, the site was relaunched, but it only consisted of a blank page with one "x" on the top left corner as the site had nothing in its source code except the single letter "x." By December, the site redirected visitors to the Boring Company's website, another one of Musk's businesses. This stunt was done to advertise a hat sale. As of now, the site went back to its original state of only displaying the blank page with the "x" in the top left corner. It is unclear if Musk has any other future plans for the site or if he just bought it out of nostalgia.

With Elon Musk, anything is possible.

---

[46] Ashlee Vance (2015), "Elon Musk: Tesla, *SpaceX, and the Quest for a Fantastic Future*," page 53.

Chapter 4: SpaceX

Elon Musk's first trademark project was SpaceX, whose "mission is to enable humans to become a spacefaring civilization and a multi-planet species by building a self-sustaining city on Mars." Space Exploration Technologies is, in fact, a private aerospace manufacturer that also offers space transportation services, founded with the ultimate goal of making space transportation more affordable so people could eventually colonize Mars. This project is very close to Elon's heart and has already managed to achieve several notable landmarks as well as develop its own launch vehicles.

His plans regarding space influenced his decision of choosing to move to Los Angeles. After the PayPal ordeal went sour, Musk went back to his childhood fantasies of rocket ships and space travel, and Los Angeles could give him the access he needed to the space industry as the weather conditions favored such ventures and all the research in the field was done somewhere around the City of Angels. Musk was not sure exactly what he was going to do, but he hoped that, in an area surrounded by top aeronautic thinkers and engineers, he would find his inspiration.

His first one-to-one connection with those "space guys" was through the Mars Society, which was dedicated to the exploration and possible future colonization of the big red planet. Musk invited himself to the society's fundraiser, where he met Robert Zubrin, the head of the society. After he double-checked to make sure that Musk had some financials backing him up, he went on to tell him all about their projects and experiments, giving him preferential treatment. It was a great chance for him to get in contact with people from this area of interest, and by the end of the night, he was a member of the Mars Society's board of directors. Robert Zubrin told Ashlee Vance his impression on the young Musk: "He was much more intense than some of the other millionaires. He didn't know a lot about space, but he had a scientific mind. He wanted to know exactly what was being planned in regard to Mars and what the significance would be."[47]

Musk, at that time, was so into the space idea that his friend feared for his mental state. He was still fresh after his malaria bout, thin and physically weak, but his determination was not faltering. The Mars Society was experimenting with mice and wished to send a few into the Earth's orbit. However, Elon Musk though they should go bigger than that. Send the mice on Mars and have them coming back, all while minding their own business and procreating. To which one of his friends responded by gifting him a giant wheel of cheese so the mice would have sufficient food for their business. He did not mind having become a laughing stock for his friends. His focus was on interplanetary travel, and NASA's plans toward such ventures were close to nonexistent. "At first I thought, jeez, maybe I'm just looking in the wrong place. Why was there no plan, no schedule? There was nothing. It seemed crazy," Musk told Wired in an interview.

He summoned all his acquired "space" contacts into a hotel conference room. He needed their help to develop his idea of bringing mice to Mars or something that could equate that, as a way of bringing the public's attention back to the red planet. The meeting resulted in Musk resigning from the Mars Society and creating his own Life to Mars Foundation. His own society gathered many talented people. Renowned scientists and celebrities alike were drawn in the dream of the red giant. One notable presence was Michael Griffin, who was the most capable person on the planet when it came to asserting the realities of space travel and whom Musk named "space thinker in chief."

The Condensed History of SpaceX

Founding

It all started with Mars Oasis, a project that Musk conceptualized in 2001. The idea was to send a mini experimental greenhouse full of seeds and dehydrated gel on Mars in order to grow life on the unfriendly Martian soil. Mars Oasis was to be a statement of how far life

---

[47] Ashlee Vance (2015), "Elon Musk: Tesla, SpaceX, and the Quest for a Fantastic Future," page 58.

can go and a means of regaining public interest in space exploration, with the slight chance of growing NASA's budget. His peers at the Life to Mars Foundation found this idea more feasible, and they already had researchers working on a space chamber that could allow plants to grow. They wanted the chamber to open, absorb Martian soil, and use that to grow the first plants on Mars and its first oxygen producers. Musk also wished that a video camera could be implemented in the structure so Earth could get footage of the plants growing and thriving on the red giant.

Dave Bearden, one of the attendees at the foundation's meetings, re-called those times when the Mars Oasis was all they could talk about: "This concept had been floating around in various forms for a while. It would be, yes, there is life on Mars, and we put it there. The hope was that it might turn on a light for thousands of kids that this place is not that hostile. Then they might start thinking, maybe we should go there."[48]

Even if the space experts admired Musk's drive, they worried about his budget. He planned to spend about $30 million on the whole ordeal, but a rocket launch could be way more costly than that. And there were also engineering challenges, like keeping the capsule warm enough for life to grow in it, which was no easy feat, especially since Musk wanted the chamber to have a big window so they could get footage. They considered using mustard seeds as the plant itself was very resilient and it had the potential to survive in the rough Martian soil. Bearden feared the effects of a failed mission: "There was a pretty big downside if the plant didn't survive. You have this dead garden on Mars that ends up giving off the opposite of the intended effect."[49]

Elon never considered giving up. Instead, Musk had an epiphany: if a new rocket technology is not invented, space travel would be exceed-ingly unaffordable for the usual person. Something needed to change. Elon took that upon himself.

---

[48] Ashlee Vance (2015), "Elon Musk: Tesla, SpaceX, and the Quest for a Fantastic Future," page 60.

[49] Ashlee Vance (2015), "Elon Musk: Tesla, SpaceX, and the Quest for a Fantastic Future," page 60.

In October that year, he traveled to Moscow alongside his best friend from college Adeo Ressi and Jim Cantrell, a mechanical engineer and aerospace supplies fixer. The group was interested in buying a Dnepr rocket to fulfill the planned launch mission. The Dnepr is a three-stage rocket that uses storable hypergolic liquid propellants and was initially used for satellite launches but was ultimately reduced to commercial use. Cantrell has previously had a bad experience with the Russians, as he was accused of espionage and placed into house arrest in 1996. He was not excited about having to deal with them again, but he obliged to Musk's plan after a rocky meeting fiasco. The two men were not very trustful of each other prior to their first face-to-face encounter. Musk was reluctant to give him his phone number and insisted on using a fax machine instead. Cantrell was afraid that Musk was working for his enemies, so he chose a secure place for the meeting where he could not "pack a gun." It all sorted out when they started talking and Cantrell understood that Musk was serious and willing to do whatever to get his rocket.

Adeo Ressi was part of Musk's group of friends that believed that he was losing his mind. They tried everything to talk him out of his plans, from showing him videos of rockets exploding to arguing that he will lose his fortune following such foolish endeavors, but nothing worked. So Adeo was on board to the Russia trip more as a guardian for Musk, out of his concern, rather than to give him advice. Cantrell told Ashlee Vance about Adeo's fears that he expressed to him whenever they were alone: "Adeo would call me to the side and say, 'What Elon is doing is insane. A philanthropic gesture? That's crazy.' He was seriously worried but was down with the trip."[50]

The men arranged meetings with companies like Lavochkin, a big player in the Russian space program and ISC Kosmotras, a joint space project that operates commercial expendable launch systems using the aforementioned Dnepr rocket. But the Russian chief designers saw Musk as nothing but an ignorant novice, and they refused any collaboration. Cantrell explained the extent of the Russians' disgust: "They

---

[50] Ashlee Vance (2015), "Elon Musk: Tesla, SpaceX, and the Quest for a Fantastic Future," page 61.

looked at us like we were not credible people. One of their chief designers spit on me and Elon because he thought we were full of shit."[51]

The group ended up returning to the United States with nothing more than disappointments. Elon was not ready to give up on his idea, so in February 2002, the group made another trip to Russia, this time bringing along Mike Griffin. At that time, Griffin was a very important figure with an impressive resume. He had worked for the CIA's venture capital arm that made sure that the agency was up to date and running the latest equipment in information technology. He was part of NASA's Jet Propulsion Laboratory project. And he was just about to leave the Orbital Sciences Corporation, which designed, manufactured, and launched satellites and spacecraft.

Their plan worked, and Kosmotras agreed to sell them one rocket for the price of US$8 million. Elon, however, did not fancy the bargain, finding the price to be too expensive, so he ended up leaving in the middle of the business meeting. According to Cantrell, Musk tried to bargain a price of $8 million for both rockets, at which the Russians scoffed: "They sat there and looked at him and said something like, 'Young boy. No.' They also intimated that he didn't have the money."[52]

Another disappointing road home turned into a eureka moment when Musk realized that he could create his own company—one that would build the affordable rockets humanity needed. Cantrell reminisced that road home when Musk first presented them with the idea of building their own rocket: "It was a long drive. We sat there in silence looking at the Russian peasants shopping in the snow. You always feel particularly good when the wheels lift off in Moscow. It's like, 'My God. I made it.' So Griffin and I got drinks and clinked our glasses."[53] At that point, Musk was sitting in front of them, vigorously tapping on his laptop. "We're thinking, fucking nerd. What can he be doing now?"[54] And to

---

[51] Ashlee Vance (2015), "Elon Musk: Tesla, SpaceX, and the Quest for a Fantastic Future," page 61.
[52] Ashlee Vance (2015), "Elon Musk: Tesla, SpaceX, and the Quest for a Fantastic Future," page 61.
[53] Ashlee Vance (2015), "Elon Musk: Tesla, SpaceX, and the Quest for a Fantastic Future," pages 61–62.
[54] Ashlee Vance (2015), "Elon Musk: Tesla, SpaceX, and the Quest for a Fantastic Future," page 62.

their surprise, Musk turned to them and cheerfully said, "Hey, guys. I think we can build this rocket ourselves."[55]

By doing some basic math, he quickly realized that, at the time, the cost of the raw materials required to build a rocket made up only 3 percent of its sales price.

To better rationalize the cost and because he believed that his concept of reusable rockets could not be turned into reality by using existing aerospace components, he applied vertical integration. He deduced that his company could cut the launch price by a factor of ten and still have the benefit of a 70 percent gross margin. He had a whole spreadsheet that detailed the costs of all materials needed along with his calculus and presented it to Cantrell and Griffin, who could not believe their eyes.

After the Russian expedition, Musk invested all his time into studying the aerospace industry. He had forgotten about his "mice in space" idea and about the Mars Oasis. He was sure that by making space exploration cheaper, he would get the public's attention. While Musk's plans made the industry buzzing with anticipation, there still were people like Zubrin, who were skeptics: "There was a string of zillionaires that got sold a good story by an engineer. Combine my brains and your money, and we can build a rocket ship that will be profitable and open up the space frontier. The techies usually ended up spending the rich guy's money for two years, and then the rich guy gets bored and shuts the thing down. With Elon, everyone gave a sigh and said, 'Oh well. He could have spent ten million dollars to send up the mice, but instead he'll spend hundreds of millions and probably fail like all the others that proceeded him.'"[56] Zubrin made the catastrophic mistake of comparing Musk to other "rich people" that saw space travel as a neat little project. For Elon Musk, it was way more than that.

SpaceX was officially founded in May 2002, its first headquarters being a 75,000 square-foot warehouse in El Segundo, California. The company was privately funded, and it developed its first "products" com-

---

[55] Ashlee Vance (2015), "Elon Musk: Tesla, SpaceX, and the Quest for a Fantastic Future," page 62.

[56] Ashlee Vance (2015), "Elon Musk: Tesla, SpaceX, and the Quest for a Fantastic Future," page 62.

pletely on private capital. Musk took the role of CEO, and Gwynne Shotwell, a savvy businesswoman and the company's eleventh employee, became its vice president of business development. Tom Muller, a rocket engine designer, was also convinced by Musk to join SpaceX as a founding employee, and he became its vice president of propulsion engineering.

Musk saw Muller as the one element that will make the difference between success and failure. Muller had a deep love for rockets since his early childhood years, and Cantrell recommended him to Musk, who went to check out his work. He found Muller in the middle of a project, and he started to bombard him with questions. "He asked me how much thrust it had. He wanted to know if I had ever worked on anything bigger. I told him that, yeah, I'd worked on a 650,000-pound thrust engine at TRW and knew every part of it."[57] Then Musk asked a price for that big engine and was not happy when Muller replied with the price that TRW built it for. Musk wanted to know for how much you could actually do it.

Muller and Musk ended up having many discussions together, and Muller helped him fill in his spreadsheet with performance and cost metrics. They wanted their rocket to fly smaller satellites, unlike the truck-sized one that everybody else was using. They focused on smaller payloads. Musk was confident that if they managed to lower the price for a rocket launch and had a regular launching schedule, a new market would open for commercial use and research. Cantrell and Griffin left SpaceX early on for fear of the risky nature of the venture.

SpaceX's goal was to make its own engines and work with suppliers for the rest of the components. It would also have to create a mobile launch vehicle that could be moved to and location and safely send the rocket to space, all those big accomplishments without SpaceX ever becoming dependent on governmental funding or on contractors.

Musk named SpaceX's first rocket, Falcon 1, a slight homage to Star Wars' Millennium Falcon. In a very bold Elon-type move, he decided that its first launch to take place only fifteen months after the company

---

[57] Ashlee Vance (2015), "Elon Musk: Tesla, SpaceX, and the Quest for a Fantastic Future," page 63.

was founded. It took a few more years for that decision to come to fruition.

Growth and Development

A lot of people liked the sound of what Musk was promising with SpaceX, regardless of Musk's unrealistic scheduling. The most excited of them all was the military. The idea of having a cheap, affordable rocket meant that they could respond to threats in space just as well as they did with at sea, on land, or in the air. In case of conflicts, they would be able to use satellites for missions, alongside many other advantages. It did not hurt that Musk looked like a reliable, determined guy. Pete Worden, a former Air Force general, described Musk: "I talked to people building ray guns and things in their garages. It was clear that Elon was different. He was a visionary who really understood the rocket technology, and I was impressed with him."[58] Medical companies and traders were also interested in the change that would be triggered by Musk's initiative.

SpaceX didn't have much room for failure, as its budget was fairly limited. Muller explained the situation to Ashlee Vance: "People thought we were just crazy. At TRW, I had an army of people and government funding. Now we were going to make a low-cost rocket from scratch with a small team. People just didn't think it could be done."[59]

Soon enough, it became clear for Musk that SpaceX would have to take care of production for all the parts, as he was not happy with what contractors had to offer. The firm announced its decision on its website: "While drawing upon the ideas of many prior launch vehicle programs from Apollo to the X-34/Fastrac, SpaceX is privately developing the entire Falcon rocket from the ground up, including both engines, the turbo-pump, the cryogenic tank structure and the guidance system. A ground-up internal development increases difficulty and the required investment, but no other path will achieve the needed improvement in the cost of access to space."[60] Fortunately, SpaceX had the team to

[58] Ashlee Vance (2015), "Elon Musk: Tesla, SpaceX, and the Quest for a Fantastic Future," page 65.

[59] Ashlee Vance (2015), "Elon Musk: Tesla, SpaceX, and the Quest for a Fantastic Future," page 66.

pull it off, such as Tim Buzza, who is a world-leading rocket tester, and Chris Thompson, who produced rockets for Boeing in the past.

In the early days of SpaceX, Mary Beth Brown joined the scene. She will go on to become one of the most important women in Musk's life—his loyal personal assistant. She was the one to express Musk's wishes to the employees and the one to take care of him in all ways possible, from managing his schedule to working extra hours alongside him whenever the case. For SpaceX, she was an important character. She tended to the smallest of details and made sure that spirits were not getting too hot. She was also the one to make the decisions in his absence. But what she was most famous for was her ability to interpret Musk's moods—something that the employees used to their advantage when it came to dealing with the boss.

In 2014, Mary Beth Brown stopped working for Musk. Allegedly, he fired her as the job required "several specialists versus one generalist."

Musk had a very ingenious idea when it came to recruiting new people for the company. He would reach out to top students from the aerospace departments of the best colleges and invite them to join over a phone call, an invitation that they were much too eager to oblige to. Engineers from companies like Boeing and Orbital Sciences were also rigged in by SpaceX's potential despite the risk. New employees were hired on a weekly basis in the first year of SpaceX's activity.

One early project that SpaceX developed was a gas generator, which is like a small gas-producing rocket engine. For its first test, the generator worked, but it produces so much black smoke that an employee of the XCOR company that was helping out urged them to stop and try another time. But the SpaceX team did not listen and just prepared everything for another test and then another. They managed to maintain a pace of multiple tests per day, and after two weeks, they had a version of the gas generator that they were happy with.

Their tests took place in Mojave, a place well known as practice location, and the team of engineers would try out many other test spots until they stumbled upon a site in McGregor that they liked so much that

---

[60] Ashlee Vance (2015), "Elon Musk: Tesla, SpaceX, and the Quest for a Fantastic Future," page 67.

they convinced Musk to acquire it. The site was abandoned after being used by others, the last being Andrew Beal, who tried to sustain an aerospace company but failed. *Rocketeers*, a book written by Michael Belfiore, explained why the site at McGregor was a gold mine for SpaceX: "After Beal saw it was going to cost him $300 million to develop a rocket capable of sending sizeable satellites into orbit, he called it quits, leaving behind a lot of useful infrastructure for SpaceX, including a three-story concrete tripod with legs as big around as redwood tree trunks."

Muller, along with Jeremy Hollman, a new employee who was disappointed with Boeing, figured out together which parts for the Falcon 1 could SpaceX make and which will it have to buy. At that time, Muller had already created computer models for the two engines that the falcon needed—Merlin, which was the bigger engine used in stage 1, and Kestrel, the smaller one that was activated in stage 2. Hollman managed the hardware by visiting machine shops. Some machinists scoffed at SpaceX's delivery times while others did their best to accommodate the company's needs. Hollman himself was not afraid to get a little creative with the parts, often choosing to recycle vehicle parts and transform them into rocket material. When the engines were done, the team wasted no time and started testing it at their new site in Texas, spending hours on end taking them apart and assessing every little piece possible.

Both engines brought along challenges. Muller explained their tests: "We would run Merlin until we ran out of hardware or did something bad. Then we'd run Kestrel and there was never a shortage of things to do. Kestrel started out as a real dog, and one of my proudest moments was taking it from terrible to great performance with stuff we bought online and did in the machine shop."[61] The engineers went on a spree with their intense schedule, something that was both stressful and "empowering," as most of them were very young, yet they were trusted to pull it off.

As well as things went most of the time, they also had bad moments, to which Musk reacted surprisingly well: "Elon had pretty good patience. I

---

[61] Ashlee Vance (2015), "Elon Musk: Tesla, SpaceX, and the Quest for a Fantastic Future," page 70.

remember one time we had two test stands running and blew up two things in one day. I told Elon we could put another engine on there, but I was really, really frustrated and just tired and mad and was kinda short with Elon. I said, 'We can put another fucking thing on there, but I've blown up enough shit today.' He said, 'Okay, all right, that's fine. Just calm down. We'll do it again tomorrow,'[62] Muller told Ashlee Vance.

While Musk could tolerate failures, he did not react well when presented with incomplete information or to a lack of planning. Hollman was the victim of Musk's temper in a situation like that: "The worst call was the first one. Something had gone wrong, and Elon asked me how long it would take to be operational again, and I didn't have an immediate answer. He said, 'You need to. This is important to the company. Everything is riding on this. Why don't you have an answer?' He kept hitting me with pointed, direct questions. I thought it was more important to let him know quickly what happened, but I learned it was more important to have all the information."[63]

Musk would often participate in tests and was not afraid to help out whenever he could in spite of his elegant demeanor or attire. In 2003, the company started to look like an actual rocket company, with a close-knit team that for many felt more like a family. SpaceX had the engines, and they were slowly developing the case that was supposed to protect the payloads. The company also managed to gain a customer, but Musk wanted to present something to people to get their interest. He wanted a prototype for the Falcon 1 ready for a public unveiling in Washington, which was due to December that year, much to the distress of the engineers who were already working crazy hours. "I think he wanted to add an element of realism to SpaceX, and if you park a rocket in someone's front yard, it's hard to deny it," Hollman gave his opinion on Musk's idea.[64]

---

[62] Ashlee Vance (2015), "Elon Musk: Tesla, SpaceX, and the Quest for a Fantastic Future," pages 70–71.

[63] Ashlee Vance (2015), "Elon Musk: Tesla, SpaceX, and the Quest for a Fantastic Future," page 71.

[64] Ashlee Vance (2015), "Elon Musk: Tesla, SpaceX, and the Quest for a Fantastic Future," page 72.

After their successful unveiling of the Falcon 1 Prototype, in 2004 the company plans focused on developing a heavy-lift product to match customer demand, each size increase resulting in a considerable decrease in cost per pound to orbit. Musk believed that "$500 per pound ($1,100/kg) or less is very achievable." They began developing the Dragon spacecraft, which they initially named Falcon 5. The main idea behind this new project was to open up the possibilities for a future NASA contract.

To keep up with this added work, Musk started another wave of hiring's, extending the company from being a one-building firm to filling up an entire complex. But more buildings meant more trouble, and the neighbors were a big part of that. In order to connect the building via fiber-optic lines, they chose a creative way of doing it—by running them through telephone poles. The SpaceX team knew it had to stick together in order to overcome the obstacles that stood in its path.

Musk always required the best from its employees, no matter what. Branden Spikes, the IT chief, knows what it means to mess up: "SpaceX's mail server crashed one time, and Elon word-for-word said, 'Don't ever fucking let that happen again.' He had a way of looking at you—a glare—and would keep looking at you until you understood him."[65] Musk was not one to favor an employee over others; he treated them all equally harsh.

Initially, he tried to find suppliers that were not exactly into the field of aerospace. He has done it in the past when SpaceX needed someone to build the body of the rocket, and he settled on companies that made big metal tanks used in agriculture. To make the fuel tanks, Musk dealt with Spincraft, a company from Wisconsin. Its failure to stick to Musk's schedule irked him so much that he made sure SpaceX could handle making the fuel tanks on its own. He had no patience for people that did not do what they were told, and he had no interest in working with people that didn't fit his standards. Many salesmen tried to sell SpaceX different technologies and went back home empty-handed.

Because of his temper, he was not liked by every single one of his employees. It was much of a "two teams" kind of situation. One adored to

---

[65] Ashlee Vance (2015), "Elon Musk: Tesla, SpaceX, and the Quest for a Fantastic Future," page 73.

be part of the company and saw Musk as a worthy leader, and the other one dabbled on his eccentricities and "injustices." One engineer declared in frustration: "The treatment of staff was not good for long stretches of this. Many good engineers, who everyone besides 'management' felt were assets to the company, were forced out or simply fired outright after being blamed for things they hadn't done. The kiss of death was proving Elon wrong about something."[66]

The year of 2004 came and went without the promised launch happening. The process was taking longer than Musk initially estimated, but by fall, the engines were fully functional and meeting all requirements. Instead of celebrating that they were closer to their goal, the engineers started to panic as problems started to unfold. "It's like anything else where you find out that the last 10 percent is where all the integration happens and things don't play together. This process went on for six months," Muller explained the phenomena.[67]

In January 2005, SpaceX purchased a 10 percent stake in Surrey Satellite Technology, a company that builds and operates small satellites. In May, they were finally ready to launch the rocket, for which they chose the Vandenberg Air Force Base. There they only managed to complete a five-second burn on the launch pads as they were not well received by the staff. "Even though they said we could fly, it was clear that we would not," Gwynne Shotwell recalled their cold attitude.[68] They had to find another site, and they chose Kwaj, as it had been used by the military before for missile testing. The challenge of moving everything to the island was not an easy one. The SpaceX team had to create its own launch pad at Omelek, a vegetation-covered island. They had problems both with accommodations and the assembly of the rocket, but they pulled through.

In November 2005, the rocket and the site were ready for the launch. Musk and his brother Kimbal came to Kawaj to witness the historic moment, but it was not meant to be. While going through the pre-launch

---

[66] Ashlee Vance (2015), "Elon Musk: Tesla, SpaceX, and the Quest for a Fantastic Future," page 74.

[67] Ashlee Vance (2015), "Elon Musk: Tesla, SpaceX, and the Quest for a Fantastic Future," page 75.

[68] Ashlee Vance (2015), "Elon Musk: Tesla, SpaceX, and the Quest for a Fantastic Future," page 75.

checks, engineers found issues with a liquid oxygen tank, which ultimately led to the cancellation of the launch altogether. They tried a second time in December, but difficulties arose a few days before the due date and plans were dropped yet again.

Musk kept investing money in the company, and by 2006, he was already US$100 million in SpaceX. The way he chose which things to fund and which not often perplexed the employees. A good example is how he refused to buy a pricey part that they believed to be essential for the rocket's success, but he did pay a similar sum to add a shiny surface to the factory floor, just to make it look better.

Finally, in March 2006, the Falcon 1 was finally ready for launch. The venture turned up to be a massive failure, with the Falcon falling back to the launching pad and the cargo smashing into the rooftop of the SpaceX machine shop. They managed to scavenge all the parts, and in a postmortem, Musk shared his opinion on the botched attempt: "It is perhaps worth noting that those launch companies that succeeded also took their lumps along the way. A friend of mine wrote to remind me that only 5 of the first 9 Pegasus launches succeeded; 3 of 5 for Ariane; 9 of 20 for Atlas; 9 of 21 for Soyuz; and 9 of 18 for Proton. Having experienced firsthand how hard it is to reach orbit, I have a lot of respect for those that persevered to produce the vehicles that are mainstays of space launch today. SpaceX is in this for the long haul, and come hell or high water, we are going to make this work."[69]

Musk wanted another launch in a span of six months, and the team of engineers tried to oblige. According to someone at the defense department, which kept tabs on their activity, the team at SpaceX lacked method: "It was being done like a bunch of kids in Silicon Valley would do software. They would stay up all night and try this and try that. I'd seen hundreds of these types of operations, and it struck me that it wouldn't work."[70]

On March 21, 2007, it finally happened. The Falcon 1 surged for the sky. "It was doing exactly what it was supposed to do. I was sitting next

[69] Ashlee Vance (2015), "Elon Musk: Tesla, SpaceX, and the Quest for a Fantastic Future," page 77.

[70] Ashlee Vance (2015), "Elon Musk: Tesla, SpaceX, and the Quest for a Fantastic Future," page 78.

to Elon and looked at him and said, 'We've made it.' We're hugging and believe it's going to make it to orbit. Then it starts to wiggle," Muller recalled the experience.[71] This time, the Falcon 1 exploded. They were close to the end of the line now, with the budget of SpaceX allowing only for about two more launch attempts.

Musk had the bad habit of protecting employees from the reality of the situation they were in. He took some harsh and maybe questionable decisions all in order to make sure that SpaceX will keep on going. Kevin Brogan, one of the early birds of SpaceX's history, explained to Ashlee Vance some of Musk's decisions and actions: "Elon would always be at work on Sunday, and we had some chats where he laid out his philosophy. He would say that everything we did was a function of our burn rate and that we were burning through a hundred thousand dollars per day. It was this very entrepreneurial Silicon Valley way of thinking that none of the aerospace engineers in Los Angeles were dialed into. Sometimes he wouldn't let you buy a part for two thousand dollars because he expected you to find it cheaper or invent something cheaper. Other times, he wouldn't flinch at renting a plane for ninety thousand dollars to get something to Kwaj because it saved an entire workday, so it was worth it. He would place this urgency that he expected the revenue in ten years to be ten million dollars a day and that every day we were slower to achieve our goals was a day of missing out on that money."[72]

It was around that time when Musk met the actor Robert Downey Jr. Downey had the upcoming role of Tony Stark, the man behind the Marvel superhero Iron Man, and in order to get more in tune with his character, he wanted to visit the SpaceX facility as it fit nicely with the film's set. When the two men had lunch, Downey was very pleased with the CEO's conduct. He had the allure and the eccentricities that would go right for his Tony Stark. "After meeting Elon and making him real to me, I felt like having his presence in the workshop. They became contemporaries. Elon was someone Tony probably hung out with and partied with or more likely they went on some weird jungle trek together to

[71] Ashlee Vance (2015), "Elon Musk: Tesla, SpaceX, and the Quest for a Fantastic Future," page 78.
[72] Ashlee Vance (2015), "Elon Musk: Tesla, SpaceX, and the Quest for a Fantastic Future," page 119.

drink concoctions with the shamans," Downey admitted.[73] He also admired Musk on a personal level as "he had seized an idea to live by" and dedicated himself to that, much like Downey did.

Also, to add to Tony Stark's cool factor, Downey asked the director of the movie, Jon Favreau, to put a Roadster in Stark's workshop and to deepen the bond between Musk and the fictional character. When the media took note that Downey's Stark was loosely based on Musk, it turned him into a more public figure. From the PayPal guy to the CEO of two innovative companies.

In that period of time, SpaceX got a contract from NASA to maintain the development and testing of the Falcon 9 launch vehicle and Dragon spacecraft. NASA was interested in using those as a means of transporting cargo to the International Space Station.

In August 2008, SpaceX got a $20 million investment from Founders Fund, a venture capital firm that focused on fields such as aerospace, artificial intelligence, energy computing, and many more.

Unfortunately, in August, they also experienced another failed launch, similar to the ladder where the Falcon 1 seemed to have made it successfully but then a malfunction struck. Dolly Singh, who was a recruiter at SpaceX at the time, recalled the incident: "It was so profound seeing the energy shift over the room in the course of thirty seconds. It was like the worst fucking day ever. You don't usually see grown-ups weeping, but there they were. We were tired and broken emotionally."[74] Musk took the stage in those moments to rally up the troops and get them back on their feet. "He said, 'Look. We are going to do this. It's going to be okay. Don't freak out.' It was like magic. Everyone chilled out immediately and started to focus on figuring out what just happened and how to fix it. It went from despair to hope and focus."[75]

By September, SpaceX already made headlines by creating the first privately funded liquid-fueled rocket that reached the orbit, a Falcon 1

[73] Ashlee Vance (2015), "Elon Musk: Tesla, SpaceX, and the Quest for a Fantastic Future," page 116.
[74] Ashlee Vance (2015), "Elon Musk: Tesla, SpaceX, and the Quest for a Fantastic Future," page 123.
[75] Ashlee Vance (2015), "Elon Musk: Tesla, SpaceX, and the Quest for a Fantastic Future," page 123.

rocket. After so many years of constant trials and failures, they finally managed to get a rocket up there. SpaceX had managed to get over its biggest hurdle and prove to the world that it was able to deliver. Musk told Ashlee Vance the speech he held for his employees after the successful launch: "Well, that was freaking awesome. There are a lot of people who thought we couldn't do it—a lot actually—but as the saying goes, 'The fourth time is the charm,' right? There are only a handful of countries on Earth that have done this. It's normally a country thing, not a company thing. . . . My mind is kind of frazzled, so it's hard for me to say anything, but, man, this is definitely one of the greatest days in my life, and I think probably for most people here. We showed people we can do it. This is just the first step of many. . . . I am going to have a really great party tonight. I don't know about you guys."[76]

In December of the same year came another contract from NASA, this time a US$1.6 billion one, for twelve flights of the Falcon 9 rocket and the Dragon spacecraft to the space station. The contract's purpose was to replace the US Space Shuttle after its retirement in 2011. SpaceX is one of two companies that have been given a contract by NASA as a part of their Commercial Resupply Services program and the Commercial Crew Development program. The goal of the second is to develop a US astronaut transport capability. Drew Eldeen, a former employee, explained why getting a NASA contract was such a huge achievement: "Traditional aerospace has been doing things the same way for a very, very long time. The biggest challenge was convincing NASA to give something new a try and building a paper trail that showed the parts were high-enough quality."[77]

On June 2009, SpaceX opened a new department: Astronaut Safety and Mission Assurance. They hired Ken Bowersox, a former NASA astronaut known for the achievement that he was the youngest person ever to command a Space Shuttle vehicle, to oversee this new addition to the company. He was appointed as vice president of Astronaut Safety and Mission Assurance, but he resigned in 2011. No public reason for the departure was given.

---

[76] Ashlee Vance (2015), "Elon Musk: Tesla, SpaceX, and the Quest for a Fantastic Future," pages 125–126.

[77] Ashlee Vance (2015), "Elon Musk: Tesla, SpaceX, and the Quest for a Fantastic Future," page 137.

Around that time, Musk made a habit out of personally interviewing every person that wanted to work for SpaceX no matter their job aspirations. Engineers and janitors alike went through the same "baptizing" performed by the CEO, a short interview that would at most last fifteen minutes. All possible future employees received a friendly warning before going through one of their most stressful encounters yet: "Elon will likely keep on writing emails and working during the initial part of the interview and not speak much. Don't panic. That's normal. Eventually, he will turn around in his chair to face you. Even then, though, he might not make actual eye contact with you or fully acknowledge your presence. Don't panic. That's normal. In due course, he will speak to you."[78]

The year 2010 came with another achievement in early December: SpaceX became the first privately funded company to successfully launch, orbit, and recover a spacecraft, meaning their Falcon 9 and Dragon.

Part of Musk's quirkiness was his habit of sending emails to all the employees when he was bothered by something or when he wanted to make changes. A 2010 email titled "Acronyms Seriously Suck" is the best and most famous example of his personal fashion of establishing an issue:

> There is a creeping tendency to use made up acronyms at SpaceX. Excessive use of made-up acronyms is a significant impediment to communication, and keeping communication good as we grow is incredibly important. Individually, a few acronyms here and there may not seem so bad, but if a thousand people are making these up, over time the result will be a huge glossary that we have to issue to new employees. No one can actually remember all these acronyms, and people don't want to seem dumb in a meeting, so they just sit there in ignorance. This is particularly tough on new employees.
>
> That needs to stop immediately, or I will take drastic action—I have given enough warnings over the years. Unless an acronym is approved by me, it should not enter the SpaceX glossary. If

[78] Ashlee Vance (2015), "Elon Musk: Tesla, SpaceX, and the Quest for a Fantastic Future," pages 134–135.

there is an existing acronym that cannot reasonably be justified, it should be eliminated, as I have requested in the past.

For example, there should be no "HTS" [horizontal test stand] or "VTS" [vertical test stand] designations for test stands. Those are particularly dumb as they contain unnecessary words. A "stand" at our test site is obviously a *test* stand. VTS-3 is four syllables compared with "tripod," which is two, so the bloody acronym version actually takes longer to say than the name!

The key test for an acronym is to ask whether it helps or hurts communication. An acronym that most engineers outside of SpaceX already know, such as GUI, is fine to use. It is also ok to make up a few acronyms/contractions every now and again, assuming I have approved them, e.g. MVac and M9 instead of Merlin 1C-Vacuum or Merlin 1C-Sea Level, but those need to be kept to a minimum.[79]

In a 2011 interview, Musk expressed his dream of sending humans to Martian soil in a time span of ten to twenty years. He remains to this day unshakable in his belief that the colonization of Mars is an achievable feat and the future of mankind.

The year 2012 was a full year for the company. By that time, SpaceX has operated on total funding of $1 billion in its first ten years, a substantial part of that sum coming from Musk himself and other investors. But contracts really started to bring the bread for SpaceX. Progress payments on launch contracts with NASA and forty launch mission contracts that came with a down payment after signing, representing a $4 billion revenue, as well as paying progress payment contracts that generated long-term revenue. In May, SpaceX became the first private company to send a spacecraft to the International Space Station. The partnership with NASA became more flourishing in August when SpaceX signed a large development contract to design and develop a crew-carrying space capsule. The purpose was to re-enable the launch of the next generation of US astronauts from American soil. Other two big companies received similar contracts from NASA. The advances made by those three will hopefully lead to making commercial human

---

[79] Ashlee Vance (2015), "Elon Musk: Tesla, SpaceX, and the Quest for a Fantastic Future," page 143.

spacecraft services available in the near future. SpaceX contract was worth $440 million for contract deliverables. In a bold move, SpaceX also advertised a launch price of $57 million, a jab at Arianespace, which promoted a $137 million price per launch. The media quickly got hold on that discrepancy, and they started commenting on the phenomenon.

Musk kept to his usual characteristic of making big ambitious promises regarding their products. As Kevin Brogan, an early SpaceX engineer explained, "Elon has always been optimistic. That's the nice word. He can be a downright liar about when things need to get done. He will pick the most aggressive time schedule imaginable assuming everything goes right, and then accelerate it by assuming that everyone can work harder."[80] But Musk was the kind of guy that worked twice as hard as he was expecting others to. He wanted to know more about their field of work, and his incredible memory made it quite simple. All he needed were willing employees that he would relentlessly question until he got the time of "knowledge" he needed. Brogan was often on the other side of this interrogation: "I thought at first that he was challenging me to see if I knew my stuff. Then I realized he was trying to learn things. He would quiz you until he learned 90 percent of what you know . . . He was teaching us about the value of time, and we were teaching him about rocketry."[81]

There was the talk of an initial public offering being possible somewhere by the end of 2013, but Musk himself decided to hold any offerings off until the BFR (Big Falcon Rocket, or as Musk called it, Big Fu*king Rocket) would be on a regular flying schedule. Later he'd come back to the subject to reiterate that there would be many years before SpaceX becomes a public company, and he prefers waiting than having it be "controlled by some private equity firm that would milk it for near-term revenue." To end all talks about going public in the midst of the company, as some employees were really hoping for the public offering to happen, Musk sent all of them an explanatory email:

---

[80] Ashlee Vance (2015), "Elon Musk: Tesla, SpaceX, and the Quest for a Fantastic Future," page 139.

[81] Ashlee Vance (2015), "Elon Musk: Tesla, SpaceX, and the Quest for a Fantastic Future," pages 138–139.

Per my recent comments, I am increasingly concerned about SpaceX going public before the Mars transport system is in place. Creating the technology needed to establish life on Mars is and always has been the fundamental goal of SpaceX. If being a public company diminishes that likelihood, then we should not do so until Mars is secure. This is something that I am open to reconsidering, but given my experiences with Tesla and Solar City, I am hesitant to foist being public on SpaceX, especially given the long-term nature of our mission.

Some at SpaceX who have not been through a public company experience may think that being public is desirable. This is not so. Public company stocks, particularly if big-step changes in technology are involved, go through extreme volatility, both for reasons of internal execution and for reasons that have nothing to do with anything except the economy.

This causes people to be distracted by the manic-depressive nature of the stock instead of creating great products. For those who are under the impression that they are so clever that they can outsmart public market investors and would sell SpaceX stock at the "right time," let me relieve you of any such notion. If you really are better than most hedge fund managers, then there is no need to worry about the value of your SpaceX stock, as you can just invest in other public company stocks and make billions of dollars in the market.[82]

Also, at that point, SpaceX became the first private company that managed to send a satellite into the geosynchronous orbit. In March 2013, SpaceX began a test program for the low-speed, low-altitude Grasshopper reusable rocket and the high-speed, high-altitude Falcon 9 booster reusable rocket. SpaceX had a slight malfunction of a Dragon spacecraft in the same month. Its fuel valves got blocked, and the craft could not function normally. Engineers managed to solve the issue, and the spacecraft successfully landed at the International Space Station with only a one-day delay.

---

[82] Ashlee Vance (2015), "Elon Musk: Tesla, SpaceX, and the Quest for a Fantastic Future," page 153.

Gwynne Shotwell said in the summer of that year that, if they managed to work out the reusable technology, the prices of the launches would drastically drop to the US$5–7 million range, something "which would really change things dramatically." In March 2014, she went further and announced that when their big spaceships, Dragon and Falcon Heavy, would be up and flying, the company will focus on developing the necessary technology to support the infrastructure required for Mars missions.

At the beginning of 2015, SpaceX raised a sum of $1 billion, consisting of founding from Google and Fidelity, a firm that invested in emerging technology companies in exchange for percentage of the company. They also accomplished the feat of sending a probe beyond Earth's orbit—the Deep Space Climate Observatory, an Earth observation satellite that additionally focused on space weather and climate.

On June 28, disaster struck. A Falcon 9, which was supposed to deliver supplies to the International Space Station, exploded due to a failed steel strut and subsequently lost its cargo—a Dragon capsule that had no parachute deployment software along with water and food supplies for the ISS. The faulty part was purchased from a supplier, and it broke due to the sheer force of acceleration. Its breach allowed the helium to escape the tanks, causing the spacecraft to explode. On the bright side, this failure led to major improvements of both the mechanical and software side, and the supplies lost were not critical—the space crew still had enough stocks to keep them going for another couple of months. Moreover, by the end of the year, SpaceX pulled off the first landing of a first-stage orbit-capable rocket, which was Falcon 9's twentieth flight.

SpaceX has grown substantially since it was founded, from 160 employees in 2005 to nearly 5,000 in February 2016. In April the same year, they had their first successful water landing of a first-stage orbit-capable rocket with, yet again, the Falcon 9.

Kevin Watson, a valuable early-day SpaceX employee, had nothing but words of praise for Elon Musk when he talked to Ashlee Vance: "Elon is brilliant. He's involved in just about everything. He understands everything. If he asks you a question, you learn very quickly not to go give him a gut reaction. He wants answers that get down to the fundamental laws of physics. One thing he understands really well is the physics of the rockets. He understands that like nobody else. The stuff I have seen him do in his head is crazy. He can get in discussions about flying a satellite and whether we can make the right orbit and deliver Dragon at the same time and solve all these equations in real time. It's amazing to watch the amount of knowledge he has accumulated over the years. I don't want to be the person who ever has to compete with Elon. You might as well leave the business and find something else fun to do. He will outmaneuver you, outthink you, and out-execute you."[83]

After facing a major setback in September 2016 consisting of their Falcon 9 Full Thrust vehicle exploding during a propellant fill operation, it took SpaceX a few months to go back to flying. The failure led to the loss of a communication satellite worth $200 million. On the bright side, there were no injuries or casualties reported. Musk considered this to be the "most difficult and complex failure" that SpaceX has ever had, and it led to an extensive investigation to find out what caused it. In November that year, Elon Musk reported that the explosion was caused by liquid oxygen, which solidified and breached the helium vessels immersed in it. Since the vessels had plenty of carbon in their composition, the solidified oxygen could have ignited it because it was under pressure, causing the explosion.

In 2017, they came full force with the successful launch of their Iridium satellites. According to *The Atlantic*, 2017 was a golden year for rocket science in the United States, and that had a lot to do with SpaceX's streak of launches. From commercial satellites to International Space Station deliveries and even some secret governmental missions, SpaceX did them all, and it excelled. Gwynne Shotwell told Space-News that the company wishes to increase its "cadence" over the years in order to eventually get to about thirty to forty launches per year.

On February 6, 2018, SpaceX launched the fourth-highest capacity rocket ever built—the Falcon Heavy, which also became the most powerful rocket to operate as of that year. The mission carried a Tesla Roadster with a dummy astronaut pilot as a humoristic payload. The

---

[83] Ashlee Vance (2015), "Elon Musk: Tesla, SpaceX, and the Quest for a Fantastic Future," page 142.

launching of a car in space became a piece of popular internet news, jokes of it appearing on numerous sites, and a reference to it being put in YouTube's 2018 Rewind. It did a wonderful job of bringing both Tesla Motors and SpaceX in the public's eyes. He followed the media ruckus with an interesting tweet in August, "SpaceX option package for new Tesla Roadster will include ~10 small rocket thrusters arranged seamlessly around car. These rocket engines dramatically improve acceleration, top speed, braking & cornering. Maybe they will even allow a Tesla to fly," keeping the buzz going.

In December, the Falcon rocket had another successful water landing, with Musk taking the time to update his twitter followers: "Engines stabilized rocket spin just in time, enabling an intact landing in water! Ships en route to rescue Falcon."

Unfortunately, in January 2019, they encountered another problem with a Falcon 9 prototype, which was ultimately supposed to take part in a Canadian satellite launch program. The rocket fell over due to strong winds and sustained damage on landing, making it impossible to recuperate the reusable components. The Canadian Space Agency announced that the project was "postponed . . . indefinitely."

SpaceX currently has a rocket development facility in Texas, which is equipped to oversee development testing in addition to testing the vehicle structure and its engines. Besides that, the facility carries on post-flight inspections and flight-proven hardware tests. Furthermore, SpaceX has four available launch sites: Vandenberg Air Force Base, Cape Canaveral Air Force Station, Kennedy Space Center (they have the privilege of using the same launch complex that was home for the Apollo and Space Shuttle programs), and SpaceX South Texas Launch Site (a record breaker, the world's first commercial launch site designed for orbital missions).

Musk is known for making big promises regarding the company's schedule, something that he seems to do regularly at both SpaceX and Tesla. He explained to Ashlee Vance his rushing nature in concordance to SpaceX's achievements: "I certainly don't try to set impossible goals. I think impossible goals are demotivating. You don't want to tell people to go through a wall by banging their head against it. I don't ever set intentionally impossible goals. But I've certainly always been optimistic on time frames. I'm trying to recalibrate to be a little more re-alistic. I don't assume that it's just like one hundred of me or something like that. I mean, in the case of the early SpaceX days, it would have been just the lack of understanding of what it takes to develop a rocket. In that case, I was off by, say, 200 percent. I think future programs might be off by anywhere from like 25 percent to 50 percent as op-posed to 200 percent. So, I think generally you do want to have a time-line where, based on everything you know about, the schedule should be X, and you execute towards that, but with the understanding that there will be all sorts of things that you don't know about that you will encounter that will push the date beyond that. It doesn't mean that you shouldn't have tried to aim for that date from the beginning because aiming for something else would have been an arbitrary time increase. It's different to say, 'Well, what do you promise people?' Because you want to try to promise people something that includes schedule margin. But in order to achieve the external promised schedule, you've got to have an internal schedule that's more aggressive than that. Sometimes you still miss the external schedule. SpaceX, by the way, is not alone here. Being late is par for the course in the aerospace industry. It's not a question of if it's late, it's how late will the program be. I don't think an aerospace program has been completed on time since bloody World War II."[84]

A Greater Goal

In Elon Musk's eyes, SpaceX is more than just a company. It's a means of preserving and expanding the consciousness of human life. Influenced by Asimov's work, he sees space exploration as the future and the only way in which humans can survive the constant threats that life on Earth implies. He further elaborates this idea: "An asteroid or a super volcano could destroy us, and we face risks the dinosaurs never saw: an engineered virus, inadvertent creation of a micro black hole, catastrophic global warming, or some as-yet-unknown technology could spell the end of us. Humankind evolved over millions of years, but in the last sixty years, atomic weaponry created the potential to ex-tinguish ourselves. Sooner or later, we must expand life beyond this

---

[84] Ashlee Vance (2015), "Elon Musk: Tesla, SpaceX, and the Quest for a Fantastic Future," pages 139–140.

green-and-blue ball—or go extinct."[85] For him, the matters are crystal clear: it's either space life or annihilation—most likely by our own hands.

Falcon 9

After SpaceX privately founded their first Falcon-type rocket, Falcon 1, which launched for only five times, the firm was ready to go back to the design board. They reused some of the structural design concepts from the Falcon 1 and ultimately created the Falcon 9, the first reusable orbital class rocket. Its development was helped by NASA funding, which saw its potential as a resupply service rocket. NASA offered a contract that provided funding for the development of both the Falcon 9 and the Dragon, as well as demonstration launches for the two space crafts. In 2008, NASA purchased twelve commercial resupply service launches to deliver cargo for the International Space Station, becoming an anchor tenant for the Falcon. Musk admitted that NASA's support was invaluable, and he publicly thanked the Commercial Orbital Transportation Services' offices for their continuous assistance and guidance provided. He also mused that he's excited to see what SpaceX will achieve in the future as a result of the partnership.

The Falcon 9 is a rocket that focuses on the transportation of satellites and the Dragon spacecraft into the Earth's orbit. It's a major accomplishment for the SpaceX team as it introduces the notion of "reusable parts," which the company believes to be the key toward a more inclusive space access and possibly could live to the inhabitation of other planets. It's designed to be reliable even in case of malfunctions, having implemented a nine first-stage engine system and minimizing risks by only having two separation events.

The launch stages are as follows:

- Interstage: Connects the first and second stages. Unlike other launch rockets, Falcon 9's stage separation system can be tested on the ground, making it more reliable.

- First stage: A special system verifies that all engines are working accordingly before release. When the thrust levels allow it, the

---

[85] *Esquire* (2008), "75 most influential people: Elon Musk."

rocket is launched to space.

- Second stage: Powered by only one engine at this point, the Falcon 9 goes in for the delivery. This engine can be reignited if there are multiple payloads to be delivered.

The star of Falcon 9 shone brightly in 2012 when it successfully delivered the Dragon spacecraft into the correct position to reach the International Space Station, putting SpaceX's name in the history books as the first private company to ever set foot on the ISS. Since its first launch, the Falcon has had plenty of successful flights, both to and from the space station or the orbit. It is not only used as a "transportation means," though. The goal of the Falcon and the Dragon alike is to deliver humans into space, as they were developed with this purpose in mind.

Dragon

Dragon is a reusable free-flying cargo spacecraft that was designed to keep both supplies and humans safe until they reach the orbiting destination. It had its first flight in 2010 when it became the first commercially built spacecraft to make it back in one piece from the orbit and is currently the only spacecraft that can bring back cargo to Earth.

The spaceship has two parts: a pressurized section and the trunk. The pressurized section is made to sustain both supplies and humans. It has honeycomb-type racks designed for maximized efficiency, which can accommodate standard NASA cargo and freezers that might be needed for biological samples. For the crew, the spacecraft will support up to seven people and will have a manual control option as well as a launch escape system. Of course, it will include the much-needed life-support system. The spaceship's pressurized section sports an advanced heat shield, a navigation and control bay, and thrusters.

The trunk can carry unpressurized cargo, and it is also the place where the solar arrays are housed. Its role is to support the spacecraft as it ascends to space.

Aside from cargo/crew transportation, Dragon can also be used as a platform fit for experiments and testing in-space technologies going by the name of Dragon Lab. It can accommodate sensor testing, microgravity testing, radiation effect search, and many others while still being able to transport experiments and instrument to and from Earth.

There are big plans for Dragon in the works as SpaceX and NASA are working toward enabling the spaceship to fly a crew. A crew test mission is planned for July 2019 and will allegedly last for fourteen days.

Falcon Heavy

Falcon Heavy is a partially reusable heavy-lift rocket deemed to be the most powerful launch vehicle in the world by a factor of two. It uses Falcon 9's data as a basis, and it adds two first stages as boosters to a strengthened core. It can lift as much as twice the payload of the next closest operational launch vehicle, and it comes at one-third of its competitor's price. Falcon Heavy was designed to get humans into space, bringing back the possibility of crew missions to fly to Mars or the Moon. It is compatible with the Dragon spacecraft.

Concepts for the Falcon Heavy were discussed as early as 2004, and SpaceX even made the bold move of announcing its first flight to be planned for 2013, at a Washington, DC, news conference. The challenges were, however, more difficult to tackle than they initially considered. Musk admittedly said, "It actually ended up being way harder to do Falcon Heavy than we thought. At first, it sounds really easy. You just stick two first stages on as strap-on boosters. How hard can that be? But then everything changes. [The loads change, aerodynamics totally change, tripled vibration and acoustics, you break the qualification levels on all the hardware, redesign the center core airframe, separation systems] . . . Really way, way more difficult than we originally thought. We were pretty naive about that."

Just as its predecessor, it's a two-stage launch vehicle.

- First stage—it comes with three cores—the main one and two boosters. One booster is equivalent to Falcon 9's first stage, having nine engines. At launch, all cores operate at full thrust. Afterward, the center one slows down while the two others separate.

- Second stage—after the separation, the rocket delivers the payload into the orbit, and the engines can be restarted for multiple deliveries, same as the Falcon 9.

Falcon Heavy is the most capable and reliable launch vehicle currently flying. Its liftoff power is equivalent to that of eighteen 747 aircrafts at full power, and those are the largest commercial planes on the market. The only rocket that surpasses Heavy Falcon in payload delivery is the Saturn V moon spacecraft, which had its last flight in 1973.

Its first flight was highly mediatized with Musk himself, building up hype by using one of his personal Tesla Roadsters as a payload, and going an extra mile by giving it a dummy pilot and a soundtrack—David Bowie's "Life on Mars." The car had cameras attached to it, and Musk later posted pictures with the "epic view." His reaction as the Falcon Heavy launched was also a memorable one: "Holy flying f——. That thing took off."

Chapter 5: Tesla, Inc.

Tesla is an energy and automotive company that specializes in electric car manufacturing. Unlike other car manufacturers and companies, Tesla does not sell its cars through dealers, but on the Web and in galleries, much like Apple. Because of this, the direct sales model is a major affront to mainstream car dealers, which are in the habit of making profits from outrageous fees. Though it was not Musk's concept, he became involved with the company in its early founding stages and is officially recognized as a co-founder. Elon Musk is the current chief executive officer of Tesla, formerly known as Tesla Motors, and his vision for the firm is to eventually make electric cars affordable for the usual customer.

Tesla Motors—the Company That Survived against All Odds

A Taken Opportunity

In July 2003, Tesla Motors made its debut on the market, initially financed and founded by Marc Tarpenning and Martin Eberhard, both being dedicated Silicon Valley engineers and savvy entrepreneurs. The decision to start Tesla Motors came to them after General Motors, the multinational corporation that dabbles in designing, manufacturing, marketing, and distributing vehicles, chose to recall all of its EV1 vehicles and destroy them. The Ev1 was the first mass-produced electric car to come from a major automaker that was also marketed under the General Motors brand instead of an affiliate. Customer reaction to the electric vehicle was mostly positive, but GM considered to niche to be unprofitable and went against customers wishes, who protested upon the termination of the model. Dave Barthmuss, the spokesman for GM, declared, "There is an extremely passionate, enthusiastic, and loyal following for this particular vehicle. There simply weren't enough of them at any given time to make a viable business proposition for GM to pursue long-term."

Tarpenning and Eberhard saw the opportunity and took it. Eberhard called a product designer, Malcolm Smith, a guy he used to work with, and allegedly said to him, "I can't tell you what we're doing, but why don't you come check out this car I have?" Smith was met with a rough business plan and an overall specifications list for their baby product—an electric car. He realized that their project was doable, but he had his doubts. Eberhard took him on a ride in their prototype—a small yellow car with a "tzero" mark on it, the mathematical symbol for the beginning. The engineer had to make Smith believe in their product. It was far more than a little experiment; it was a real vehicle with a lot of technicalities to it. When he witnessed the real power of the yellow electric car—it could jump from 0 to 60 in under four seconds—he was hooked. That's how Smith became the vice president of vehicle engineering for Tesla Motors and one of the firm's first employees.

Ian Wright, the first vice president of vehicle development that Tesla Motors had, was very taken with their "tzero" prototype too. He made three main points about why the car had so much raw potential:

- The power of the card did not fade as it accelerated.
- The power control was intuitive and simple to get accustomed to.
- The speed control was easy and precise even at parking speeds.

Tarpenning was sick of hearing the media claim that "electric cars would never succeed" because of a lack of development in the battery industry, but that was only true of acid batteries. The young team veered toward lithium-ion batteries. They were "cheaper and better," more so as time went by. Eberhard and Tarpenning had no knowledge regarding building cars, but they realized that the automotive world was low-key open for start-up companies. They did their homework diligently and ultimately decided to go for their goals and create the first exclusively electric car company. They settled on the name Tesla Motors as an homage to the Serbian-American inventor Nikola Tesla. The idea of an electric car was frowned upon even by people that knew them. "We met a friend at this Woodside pub to tell her what we had finally decided to do and that it was going to be an electric car. She said, 'You have to be kidding me,'"[86] related Tarpenning.

Tesla Motors started with the primary focus of commercializing a premium electric sports car to please early adopters. After that, they planned to slip into more mainstream vehicles, such as sedans and affordable compacts. The engineers at Tesla Motors realized that it was a lot easier to build on top of a car that was already made, so they settled for the Elise model manufactured by Lotus because it was a sports car and the British firm had an affordable rate compared to other bigger car makers, like Ford or Porsche. In 2003, at an auto show that took place in Los Angeles, they got in touch with the Lotus Team and offered them a ride on the prototype.

Musk Enters the Game

Musk joined the company in 2004 as an early-stage investor as well as a chairman. Eberhard and Tampering met him back in 2001 at a Mars Society conference. They made him an offer via email: "We would love to talk to you about Tesla Motors, particularly if you might be interested in investing in the company. I believe that you have driven AC Propulsion's tzero car. If so, you already know that a high-performance electric car can be made. We would like to convince you that we can do so profitably, creating a company with very high potential for growth and at the same time breaking the compromise between driving performance and efficiency."[87] To which he replied with a simple "Sure." Eberhard and Wright went to Musk's office at the SpaceX Company and presented their concept in a two-hour pitch meeting. Even if Elon Musk was sympathetic with their goals, he still had his doubts regarding the costs of design and production. He eventually relented after a final meeting, this time with Tarpenning, with his only preference being that they "do it quick." At that time, his wife was pregnant with twins, and he would soon not have the time necessary to "deal" with them. "You need angel investors to have some belief, and it wasn't a purely financial

---

[86] Ashlee Vance (2015), "Elon Musk: Tesla, SpaceX, and the Quest for a Fantastic Future," page 101.

[87] Drake Baer (2014), "The Making of Tesla: Invention, Betrayal, and the Birth of the Roadster," *Business Insider.*

transaction for him. He wanted to change the energy equation of the country," Tarpenning explained Musk's motivation.[88]

Although he had a mainly active role in the company and got himself involved in the Roaster's (the first vehicle they manufactured) design, he was not up to date with the company's everyday business operations. He was, however, the controlling investor, founding most of the first series capital investment road, and he maintained a high interest in the company product development. Musk was the one that insisted on going for a carbon-fiber-reinforced polymer body, and he overviews styling and operational decisions. He also made it very clear for anyone that wanted to listen that Tesla's future goal was set on mass production of affordable electric vehicles.

Along with Musk, J. B. Straubel joined the team. He was a physics with a great interest in clean technology, especially cars. He wanted to create an electric car, and he had met Musk in the past to present his lithium-ion battery concept. "Everyone else had told me I was nuts, but Elon loved the idea. He said, 'Sure, I will give you some money,'"[89] Straubel reminisced his first meeting with Musk. Elon kept his word and offered him $10,000 to keep on developing the battery. When it came to joining Tesla, Musk called Straubel to stop by the office. "I told them that I had been building the battery pack they need down the street with funding from Elon. We agreed to join forces and formed this ragtag group," Straubel told Ashlee Vance.[90] Thanks to Straubel's influence in the field, Tesla soon had plenty of young engineers on hand, ready to give it their all for the project of their life.

Ian Wright believed that working with Lotus turned up to be very beneficial for Tesla Motors, and he did his best to keep their partnership going smooth. They learned many important lessons, such as how seemingly simple parts can turn out to be much more difficult to manage with intricate steps and a bunch of possible issues. The design could not be sacrificed, but neither did functionality—all by sticking to tolerable vari-

---

[88] Ashlee Vance (2015), "Elon Musk: Tesla, SpaceX, and the Quest for a Fantastic Future," page 102.

[89] Ashlee Vance (2015), "Elon Musk: Tesla, SpaceX, and the Quest for a Fantastic Future," page 99.

[90] Ashlee Vance (2015), "Elon Musk: Tesla, SpaceX, and the Quest for a Fantastic Future," pages 102–103.

ations. Wright concluded that "all these things that we thought were easy were really not that easy. We didn't know anything about building cars."[91] Wright also managed to secure with AC Propulsions, the manufacturers of the tzero, before amicably leaving the company.

The Roadster

The Tesla Roadster was the company's first vehicle. It's a battery-electric sports car that was based on a Lotus Elise, a two-seat, mid-engine roadster manufactured by Lotus Cars in the '90 chassis.

In the original executive summary of Tesla's business plan, the Roadster's promised vitals were as follows:

- zero emissions
- easy intuitive handling
- the possibility to go from 0 to 60 in 3.9 seconds
- to match a 100-mile-per-gallon vehicle
- a range of 300 miles
- a guaranteed 100,000 miles that did not require maintenance (except for tires)
- an affordable selling price

Malcolm Powell, who was a long-time Lotus employee, had many doubts regarding the Roadster's initial design. He would later declare to the *Business Insider*: "Most people outside of the industry have little idea how complex and difficult it is to design and develop a production vehicle, even one using conventional technology. Don't forget, at that time, no one was making a high-performance electric vehicle, nor was anyone achieving adequate range. Their product was, therefore, out of the ordinary." For a couple of months though, Powell became the vice president of vehicle integration for Tesla Motors, as he knew the Elise in and out, and also acted as a link between Tesla and Lotus. The British company was very careful with those beginners that had no idea what they were doing because they did not want to tarnish their or their

---

[91] Drake Baer (2014), "The Making of Tesla: Invention, Betrayal, and the Birth of the Roadster," *Business Insider*.

product's reputation. As a consequence, Lotus had the last word in anything they were doing as partners.

The Roadster was something new—made out of Tesla's own technology along with random parts available in the auto manufacturer's field, which meant both endless opportunities and problems. Eberhard knew how he wanted the Roadster to look and feel, but he had no idea how to make the designers understand his vision. Eberhard needed help, so he called upon a longtime friend of his, Bill Moggridge, a somewhat legendary designer, one of his biggest credited invention being the styling of the first modern laptop. He helped Eberhard realize exactly what he wanted for the Roadster:

- A retro look which would fit a sports car
- A design that would appeal both to men and women alike
- A somewhat curvaceous design, something close to older Ferraris, with a little bit of a modern vibe

With Moggridge's presentation at hand, people finally understood Eberhard's concept. He narrowed it down to four final designs. On that year's Christmas party, he invited the whole Tesla team, along with their families, to his house in San Mateo County. Musk, however, could not attend. Even so, Eberhard used the opportunity to decide once and for all the final Roadster Design. He gave his guests green and red Post-it notes to attach to the pictures that showed the possible Roadsters. Green meant they liked it, and red was counted as a negative opinion. One design stood out, that of Barney Hatt, who was the chief designer at Lotus, and so, the Roadster found a look to attach to its name.

In November 2004, they got the first real Tesla going—an Elise full of their technology. "The original plan had been to do the bare minimum we could get away with as far as making the car stylistically different from a Lotus but electric. Along the way, Elon and the rest of the board said, 'You only get to do this once. It has to delight the customer, and the Lotus just isn't good enough to do that," Tarpenning reminisced about the early days of the Roadster.[92]

---

[92] Ashlee Vance (2015), "Elon Musk: Tesla, SpaceX, and the Quest for a Fantastic Future," page 105.

It had no body panels, but it came with software, hardware, and a revised battery. Only that, but it still was able to "rocket down the pavement" as it was. Smith would later say when recalling the first actual ride of a Tesla-branded vehicle: "The first fully functioning mule was the real proof of concept and would lead us to the production design. Any time you have some new tech that you're not sure is going to work or not, you get a little bit of that Wright brothers feeling—it did get off the ground."[93]

The year 2006 was the year when people started finding out about the Roadster. It was shown for the first time at the Barker Hangar in Santa Monica. A day full of "complete panic" and excitement. The guests were pre-amatively announced that they would have the chance to pre-order one of the first 100 Tesla Roadster ever made—a marketing move that proved successful. Hollywood names like Michael Eisner and Arnold Schwarzenegger popped in. Test drives started, and the process was so intense that both cars that were for the show had the upper motor mount broken by the end of the day—an issue, a small issue that did not affect their performance. Ebner later said, "From the audience's perspective, they didn't have a problem. Anybody who got into one of those cars had their opinion of electric cars instantly changed."[94]

At the event, both Musk and Eberhard said a few words, but the later made a bigger impression. By then, Elon Musk was a fresh name with not much of a cult following. Being still at the start of his career and, according to Casner, one of Eberhard's friends, "Elon's ability to speak in public and convey the sense of the company was not nearly as good as what Martin had done. I don't know if it's a matter of what language is used or colorful phrases. He just didn't seem to be nearly as effective in making people excited and believe in this trend."[95] Eberhard was then the Tesla icon, and he managed interviews better than anyone at the company. They even worked out great, and Tesla Motors managed

[93] Drake Baer (2014), "The Making of Tesla: Invention, Betrayal, and the Birth of the Roadster," *Business Insider*.

[94] Drake Baer (2014), "The Making of Tesla: Invention, Betrayal, and the Birth of the Roadster," *Business Insider*.

[95] Drake Baer (2014), "The Making of Tesla: Invention, Betrayal, and the Birth of the Roadster," *Business Insider*.

to sell 127 Roadsters. The firm was careful with their marketing strategy and made sure to keep all fields open by not limiting themselves to the automobile press. Everywhere you look, you'd end up with some Tesla news, most of it being positive. The *Washington Post* made it clear that Tesla's try at an electric vehicle was not "your father's electric car. The $100,000 vehicle, with its sports car looks, is more Ferrari than Prius—and more about testosterone than granola."

All the attention was fixated on Eberhard as he was "the man with the idea." Musk felt that his own involvement was downplayed, and he released a statement to better explain his position at Tesla Motors: "The way that my role has been portrayed to date, where I am referred to merely as 'an early investor' is outrageous. That would be like Martin [Eberhard] being called an 'early employee.' Apart from me leading the Series A and B and co-leading the Series C, my influence on the car itself runs from the headlights to the styling to the door sill to the trunk, and my strong interest in electric transport predates Tesla by a decade. Martin should certainly be the front and center guy, but the portrayal of my role to date has been incredibly insulting. I'm not blaming you or others at Tesla—the media is difficult to control. However, we need to make a serious effort to correct this perception."[96] The *New York Times* kept overseeing Musk again and again, which only infuriated Musk further. He and Eberhard managed to get over this conflict, but Musk announced that he'd step aside from Tesla if his merits won't be acknowledged.

After it was done with marketing, Tesla went back to developing the car. The third Roadster prototype went to a collision testing facility to see how it would do in crash situations. The facility was one used by the biggest automakers, so Tesla had access to top-notch imaging technologies and to computer simulations. That meant a lot to a company that could not afford to build an army of prototypes just to have them crashed. Tesla also had access to durability tracks that could emulate ten years of wear for the car. Unlike other car manufacturers, Tesla sent its engineers along with the cars on the tests to analyze

---

[96] Drake Baer (2014), "The Making of Tesla: Invention, Betrayal, and the Birth of the Roadster," *Business Insider.*

data on the spot. If any tweaks of modifications were needed, they could do them immediately and send the car back on the track.

Some of the engineers saw Musk as a troublemaker, as he always made changes that delayed the car from being shipped. "It felt at times like Elon was this unreasonably demanding overarching force. The company as a whole was sympathetic to Martin because he was there all the time, and we all felt the car should ship sooner," one of them told Ashlee Vance.[97]

In 2006, Elon Musk received the Global Green product design award for the Tesla Roadster, and in 2007, he received the Index Design award for the same concept. Finally, he was getting some credit for his involvement in the Roadster's creation.

Tesla was steadily growing and achieving the impossible. It seemed like all that kept them from succeeding was their own ambition and approach. They were in the place where they had to build cars, a process that almost ended up shutting the company down. One of the biggest mistakes was the way they dealt with the transmission system of the Roadster. The car had to go from 0 to 60 mph as fast as possible; that was always a focal point for the company. "People had been making transmissions since Robert Fulton built the steam engine. We thought you would just order one. But the first one we had lasted forty seconds," explained Bill Currie, an engineer and early employee of Tesla.[98]

Soon enough, it became clear that the contractors that Tesla hoped would produce their transmissions were not that interested in helping a small company. The replacements they offered were just as faulty as the initial ones. Tesla initially planned to start delivering the Roadster by the end of 2007, but the problem with the transmission persisted. At the beginning of 2008, Tesla was forced to abandon all their previous ideas regarding the transmission system and rethought the issue.

Besides problems with the car, Tesla also had setbacks with their battery factory that they had in the works in Thailand. But the Thai manufactures were not at all ready to handle the sensitive batteries and elec-

---

[97] Ashlee Vance (2015), "Elon Musk: Tesla, SpaceX, and the Quest for a Fantastic Future," page 107.

[98] Ashlee Vance (2015), "Elon Musk: Tesla, SpaceX, and the Quest for a Fantastic Future," page 108.

tronics that they had. Tesla engineers had to teach them everything from scratch while also supervising the building process of the factory. The development of the battery was going slower than ever.

The whole plan that Tesla had in mind for producing the car was ambitious if not completely insane. It involved a global venture: body panels made in France, motors in Taiwan, battery cells from China, and the battery pack was to be finished off in England. As a consequence, the Roadster's production was prone to delays. "The idea was to get to Asia, get things done fast and cheap, and make money on the car. What we found out was that for really complicated things, you can do the work cheaper here and have less delays and less problems," explained Forrest North, a Tesla engineer.[99]

Musk was worried that the manufacturing issues were dragging the company down, so he called Tim Watkins, who was a managing director of operations at Valor Equity, to assess the situation. While the employee costs were not an issue, according to Watkins's findings, the manufacturing process was a disaster. Musk recalled the unpleasant episode: "That's when Tim told me it was really bad news. Even in full production, they would have been like $170,000 or something insane. Of course, it didn't much matter because about a third of the cars didn't flat-out fucking work."[100] Watkins concluded that it would take about $200,000 to produce one Roadster while the intended sales price was $85,000.

To rally up his team of engineers, Eberhard called them into the main workshop and gave them a speech inspired by the one that John Doerr had made, advocating for the future of the Earth and the use of green energy. He projected a picture of his daughter on the wall and spoke to them fervently. "We are building this because by the time she is old enough to drive, she will know a car as something completely different to how we know it today, just like you don't think of a phone as a thing on the wall with a cord on it. It's this future that depends on you," he told them to remind them of the bigger purpose behind Tesla.[101] "We were all working ourselves to the point of exhaustion. Then came this

---

[99] Ashlee Vance (2015), "Elon Musk: Tesla, SpaceX, and the Quest for a Fantastic Future," page 109.
[100] Ashlee Vance (2015), "Elon Musk: Tesla, SpaceX, and the Quest for a Fantastic Future," pages 109–110.

profound moment where we were reminded that building the car was not about getting to an IPO or selling it to a bunch of rich dudes, but because it might change what a car is," said an ex-employee regarding the effect of Eberhard's speech.[102]

In 2009, the Roadster set a world distance record for achieving 501 kilometers on a single charge at the speed of 40 km/h. In March 2010, it set another record by becoming the first electric vehicle to win the Monte Carlo Alternative Energy Rally and the first that won a sanctioned championship of the Federation Internationale de l'Automobile when its driver Erik Comas beat all his competitors on all categories—range, efficiency, and performance.

It's the first highway-legal all-electric car and also the first to travel more than 320 km per change. The Roadster uses lithium-ion battery cells, and it was met with a fair amount of excitement. It was sold in over thirty countries, and it qualified for governmental incentives—a worldwide movement that supports the adoption of plug-in electric vehicles that offers different perks to customers that opt for emission-free cars—in several nations.

Thanks to Musk's close affiliation with SpaceX, the Tesla Roadster was forever marked in history books as the first production car to be launched into orbit during the first flight of the Falcon Heavy.

On rocky grounds

Tesla Motors initially had four rounds of investments. Series A had Musk as the lead investor, with US$7.5 million of his personal funds going in the company's capital, and it included other important supporters, such as Compass Technology Partners and SDL Ventures. Series B as well was led by Musk with US$13 million, and it added Valor Equity Partners to the invertor's team. Technology Partners and Elon Musk co-led the third round with the sum of US$40 million. The third round brought along some big investors, like Jeff Skoll (the former president of eBay), Google co-founders Sergey Brin and Larry Page, and many others. The Bay Area Equity Fund and a couple of VC firms

[101] Ashlee Vance (2015), "Elon Musk: Tesla, SpaceX, and the Quest for a Fantastic Future," page 110.
[102] Ashlee Vance (2015), "Elon Musk: Tesla, SpaceX, and the Quest for a Fantastic Future," page 110.

joined in too. The fourth and final round added a sum of US$45 million, all in private funding.

The shipment of the Roadster was supposed to start in 2006, but the actual shipment of it started in early 2008. In October that year, Musk told Eberhard in an email that Tesla Motors had only two viable options: "sacrifice a six-month first mover advantage in a market that is like the internet circa 1992 (but slower-moving) or focus every bit of energy on getting our product right."[103] Eberhard responded that he had worries of his own regarding the Roadster and that he feared that it could be postponed to the year 2007, despite his promise.

From there on, things only became more complicated. Production was supposed to be "low-cost" with Lotus handling most of it, as well as making sure the end product did not look like a Lotus itself. Originally, Tesla was supposed to add only five parts of the car—mostly assemblies that would be bolted on, as well as the battery pack subassembly. From those five pieces, they ended up adding hundreds of tweaks. Musk had a lot to do with most of the modifications. He wished for lower door sills, bespoke headlights, a quality dashboard material, and more comfortable seats. And then, there was the transmission, which "is not an inherently difficult item, but if you have two suppliers screw the pooch on you, then you're looking at some tardiness."[104]

Eberhard did not expect Tesla Motors to have to supply so many components to Lotus, and the company was not ready for that commitment. The firm was getting bigger at an alarming pace, and everything was going downhill. They had problems with their finances, and they also had to change the bookkeeping to the enterprise software management, both feats exceeding Eberhard's abilities. Tesla needed a new CEO, one with more experience, and Musk agreed. So did the Tesla team. According to Eberhard, they thanked him for his services and wished for him to stay as an advisor and technician. In that time, Musk had to visit Lotus HQs, all on his own, to see how production was going and to assure the firm that Tesla was financially capable of bringing the

---

[103] Drake Baer (2014), "The Making of Tesla: Invention, Betrayal, and the Birth of the Roadster," *Business Insider.*

[104] Drake Baer (2014), "The Making of Tesla: Invention, Betrayal, and the Birth of the Roadster," *Business Insider.*

Roadster to the market. Unfortunately, they were already behind schedule and worried sick that issues kept coming.

Eberhard focused so much on the engineering team that he unwillingly ignored other important facets of Tesla. His decisions were bringing Tesla down. "Everyone knew that the person who starts a company is not necessarily the right person to lead it in the long term, but whenever that is the case, it's not easy," an employee told Ashlee Vance.[105]

Musk was alarmed by the situation at Lotus and allegedly wrote in an e-mail: "There are several burning Roadster issues that need Martin's attention right now. We have slipped delivery significantly already and are at risk of slipping even more. I feel strongly that Martin should minimize any optional activity, particularly low to moderate value PR and finance meetings, and focus on company execution, which will have a major effect on our financing and valuation."[106] Elon Musk was still on speaking terms with Eberhard, but his responsibility in the Roadster's delays can't be ignored. Despite his valuable inputs regarding design and style, he was not very present in the office. He's inconsistency caused delays and disrupted workflow, to everyone's frustration. According to employees, Musk came with "good reasoning," but he could not deliver his feedback in real time.

However, the board considered that Eberhard did not succeed in portraying the real severity of the situation, so in 2007, he was denoted.

While the delays kept happening, Tesla Motors was also on the lookout for a new CEO. No one was good enough to take up the spot left empty by Eberhard, including the Tesla man himself. The media got involved, presenting Eberhard as a victim. That got Musk furious, and he reminded the ex-CEO who went over to express at a conference that he was forced out of the firm, that his claim to be fired was nothing but a misconception. "The objective fact is you brought up the CEO search yourself several months ago," Musk reminded him.[107] Ultimately, Musk announced to Eberhard that he has been replaced by Michael Marks,

---

[105] Ashlee Vance (2015), "Elon Musk: Tesla, SpaceX, and the Quest for a Fantastic Future," page 110.

[106] Drake Baer (2014), "The Making of Tesla: Invention, Betrayal, and the Birth of the Roadster," *Business Insider*.

[107] Drake Baer (2014), "The Making of Tesla: Invention, Betrayal, and the Birth of the Roadster," *Business Insider*.

the ex-CEO of Flextronics, to which the other retaliated by claiming that he was not informed in time by the change and that he did not get the chance to defend his position. Eberhard consulted his lawyer, and with his help, he convinced the board to have another meeting, which allowed him to step down by his own will and take the title of president of technology.

However, Eberhard was in charge of peripheral issues and troubleshooting and nothing else. Eberhard still managed to elevate the company's issues with his conduct. "Martin was so bitter and disruptive. I remember him running around the office and sowing discontent as we're trying to finish the car and are running out of money and everything is at knife's edge," Straubel described Eberhard in his new function.[108] He tried to find excuses for the delays and bad financials that would exonerate him of blame, and he also contested Watkins's findings. "Valor was used to dealing with older companies. They found chaos and weren't used to it. This was the chaos of a start-up," he argued.[109]

When he had enough, he quit, making declarations that he was treated unfairly. The company shunned him, and Musk took over. He made a statement of his own, explaining to the public Eberhard's departure from Tesla: "I'm sorry that it came to this and wish it were not so. It was not a question of personality differences, as the decision to have Martin transition to an advisory role was unanimous among the board. Tesla has operational problems that need to be solved, and if the board thought there was any way that Martin could be part of the solution, then he would still be an employee of the company."[110]

Harrigan, the vice president of marketing, explained by admitting that Elon Musk was that sort of boss: "Once he's convinced that you can't do the job, there's no way you can convince him back again. That happened many times to many people, and that's what happened with

[108] Ashlee Vance (2015), "Elon Musk: Tesla, SpaceX, and the Quest for a Fantastic Future," page 110.

[109] Ashlee Vance (2015), "Elon Musk: Tesla, SpaceX, and the Quest for a Fantastic Future," page 111.

[110] Ashlee Vance (2015), "Elon Musk: Tesla, SpaceX, and the Quest for a Fantastic Future," page 111.

Martin. Once he determined that Martin couldn't be the CEO of Tesla any longer, that was it. He was fired."[111]

Problems kept piling up with the development of the Roadster. The motor malfunctioned regularly. The body panels had gaps, and the carbon fiber body that Musk adored was very picky when it came to paint. By that time, Tesla had also given up on the two-speed transmission idea as it continued to fail. According to Musk, in order to get the car to work, they had to make "a complete reboot," a redesigned motor, and many other tweaks.

The new CEO made a good impression. Straubel described him in high notes: "Martin had been falling apart and lacked a lot of the discipline key for a manager. Michael came in and evaluated the mess and was a bullshit filter. He didn't really have a dog in the fight and could say, 'I don't care what you think or what you think. This is what we should do.'"[112]

However, Marks was just a temporary solution, as he knew nothing about electric vehicles. He filled in the spot at Musk's request and nothing more. The company was very affected by Eberhard's leave, and the ex-CEO's relationships with Musk were strained. Things were terrible for Tesla, and Marks did his best to mend whatever he could. According to him, he did three important things to keep Tesla rolling.

1. He stopped a $30 million shipments of parts because the product design was not ready.

2. He cut out Tesla's R & D services.

3. He created a list of over thirty items that had to be completed before the Roadster could be shipped.

But Marks also inclined toward transforming Tesla into an asset that could benefit a larger company rather than make it work on its own. For Marks, it seemed like the most logical approach. "The product was late and over budget, and everything was wrong, but Elon didn't want anything to do with those plans to either sell the whole company or lose

---

[111] Drake Baer (2014), "The Making of Tesla: Invention, Betrayal, and the Birth of the Roadster," *Business Insider.*

[112] Ashlee Vance (2015), "Elon Musk: Tesla, SpaceX, and the Quest for a Fantastic Future," page 111.

control through a partnership. So Elon decided to double down," Straubel explained.[113]

In December 2007, Ze'ev Drori became president and CEO, replacing Michael Marks. This replacement led to a series of personnel reduction in 2008, a couple of key employees being fired after a performance review made by the new CEO. Musk backed up this decision, affirming that Tesla had to reduce its workforce in order to cut the burn rate, which was previously "out of control."

There was a lot of negative press about Tesla at the time—a trend that never died out completely—so Musk wrote a blog post to remind the public that Tesla was still there: "Given the recent management changes, some reassurances are in order regarding Tesla Motors' future plans. The near term message is simple and unequivocal—we are going to deliver a great sports car next year that customers will love driving. . . . My car, production VIN 1, is already off the production line in the UK, and final preparations are being made for importation."[114] Despite the repeated delays, most customers still waited patiently for their cars to arrive.

Elon started to get involved firsthand into the production process of the car, and he became the "fussy tyrant" that SpaceX employees knew much too well. He wanted to know everything to the very last detail, and nothing was allowed to be ambiguous. Popple, an employee at Tesla, told Ashlee Vance about Musk's leadership methods: "Elon got fired up and said we were going to do this intense cost-down program. He gave a speech, saying we would work on Saturdays and Sundays and sleep under desks until it got done. Someone pushed back from the table and argued that everyone had been working so hard just to get the car done, and they were ready for a break and to see their families. Elon said, 'I would tell those people they will get to see their families a lot when we go bankrupt.' I was like, 'Wow,' but I got it. I had come out of a military culture, and you just have to make your objective happen."[115]

---

[113] Ashlee Vance (2015), "Elon Musk: Tesla, SpaceX, and the Quest for a Fantastic Future," page 112.
[114] Ashlee Vance (2015), "Elon Musk: Tesla, SpaceX, and the Quest for a Fantastic Future," page 112.

Musk's main goal was to make sure that all costs were cut as drastically as possible. And he had no patience for those who were too slow in delivering results. "If you started falling behind, there was hell to pay. Everyone could see it, and people lost their jobs when they didn't deliver. Elon has a mind that's a bit like a calculator. If you put a number on the projector that does not make sense, he will spot it. He doesn't miss detail. Some people thought Elon was too tough or hot-tempered or tyrannical. But these were hard times, and those of us close to the operational realities of the company knew it. I appreciated that he didn't sugarcoat things," Popple reminisced, half fearful, half in admiration.[116]

His harshness has no boundaries. Marketing people were tasked with "fixing" any negative Tesla story that was out there. Mistakes and delays were not tolerated. He would fire people just for making grammatical mistakes in emails or for simply not doing something "grand" in a period of time. "He can be incredibly intimidating at times but doesn't have a real sense for just how imposing he can be. We'd have these meetings and take bets on who was going to get bloodied and bruised. If you told him that you made a particular choice because 'it was the standard way things had always been done,' he'd kick you out of a meeting fast. He'd say, 'I never want to hear that phrase again. What we have to do is fucking hard, and half-assing things won't be tolerated.' He just destroys you, and if you survive, he determines if he can trust you. He has to understand that you're as crazy as he is," recalled a former Tesla executive.[117]

Many employees left because they were too tired to keep on fighting for a dream that, with each day that went by, seemed less and less achievable. Eberhard was gone, so Tarpenning followed. And so did other early employees, although most of them still hold Elon into high regards. "Don't worry about the methods or if they're unsound. Just get the job done. It comes from Elon. He listens, asks good questions, is fast on his feet, and gets to the bottom of things," one former Tesla

---

[115] Ashlee Vance (2015), "Elon Musk: Tesla, SpaceX, and the Quest for a Fantastic Future," page 113.

[116] Ashlee Vance (2015), "Elon Musk: Tesla, SpaceX, and the Quest for a Fantastic Future," page 113.

[117] Ashlee Vance (2015), "Elon Musk: Tesla, SpaceX, and the Quest for a Fantastic Future," page 113.

member described him.[118] Straubel was one of the few that stayed as he understood the importance of an electric vehicle. For him, it only mattered to bring that dream to life, and Musk seemed like the person that could do it. He remained loyal to Tesla and its mission.

In 2008, Tesla needed another investment round in order to keep on going, and the website "The Truth about Cars" launched a "Tesla Death Watch." News outlets were fuming—Tesla was going down. Critics were tearing it down, saying that they "couldn't produce cars" or that "no one wanted their cars." The automotive industry did not like the start-up business or its first initiative, the Roadster. Top Gear went as far as to make it seem like the car was easily running out of energy without giving proper warnings. Big techs and car outlets saw Tesla as nothing but a joke. All the more to motivate Tesla to go on following their dreams. Musk was the one that had to convince the investors that Tesla was worth it. "Try to imagine explaining that you're investing in an electric car company, and everything you read about the car company sounds like it is shit and doomed and it's a recession and no one is buying cars," he put the situation into perspective for Ashlee Vance.[119]

Musk took the reigns as the CEO in October that year and went on to fire 25 percent of the employees. He explained his newfound position by saying, "I've got so many chips on the table with Tesla. It just made sense for me to have both hands on the wheel."[120] The change of CEO gave Valleywag, the gossip site, fuel for its fire. Not only it ridiculed Tesla for the shift in power, but it also published an alleged report from an employee that pictured the company to be in a bad financial situation. More than the bad financials, it claimed that Tesla was actually scamming its customers. "We have over 1,200 reservations, which manes [sic] we've taken multiples of tens of millions of cash from our customers and have spent them all," the Tesla employee wrote. "Meanwhile, we only delivered less than fifty cars. I actually talked a close

---

[118] Ashlee Vance (2015), "Elon Musk: Tesla, SpaceX, and the Quest for a Fantastic Future," page 114.

[119] Ashlee Vance (2015), "Elon Musk: Tesla, SpaceX, and the Quest for a Fantastic Future," page 114.

[120] Drake Baer (2014), "The Making of Tesla: Invention, Betrayal, and the Birth of the Roadster," *Business Insider.*

friend of mine into putting down $60,000 for a Tesla Roadster. I cannot conscientiously be a bystander anymore and allow my company to deceive the public and defraud our dear customers. Our customers and the general public are the reason Tesla is so loved. The fact that they are being lied to is just wrong."[121] The employee was later discovered, and he willingly resigned after issuing an apology.

Luckily in December, they got another round of funding of US$40 million, which put a stop to the Tesla Death Watch once and for all.

In May 2009, Daimler A. G., the maker of Mercedes-Benz, acquired an approximately 10 percent equity stake of Tesla for US$50 million. In a matter of a few months, Aabar Investments purchased 40 percent of Daimler's interest. Still, in the year of 2009, Tesla Motors received a US$465 million loan from the United States Department of Energy. It supported both the engineering and the production of their next vehicle, the Model S sedan, and the development of powertrain technology for commercial use. In August of 2009, they announced that they managed to achieve overall corporate profitability, which earns close to US$1 million on revenue of US$20 million. The profit mostly came from the 2010 Roaster's sales, the second version of their baby project. They sold 109 vehicles in July, a record for Tesla Motors. Still in the year of 2009, Musk recalled most of the old Roadsters, and technicians were sent to fix issues as the cars had let a few people down, including high-maintenance celebrities like George Clooney, who actually chose to sell his Tesla. As a reason, he stated that he would always end up "on the side of the road." Musk retaliated on his Twitter page by saying, "In other news, George Clooney reports that his iPhone 1 had a bug back in '07," showcasing that the actor had no idea what a novelty item the Roadster actually was and how issues were to be expected.

Going Public

At the beginning of 2010, Tesla Motors wanted to become public and filed a preliminary prospectus to affirm its intention to make a stock market launch. Tesla announced its offer on the Nasdaq Stock Market, issuing over 13K shares of stock to the public, which eventually raised

---

[121] Ashlee Vance (2015), "Elon Musk: Tesla, SpaceX, and the Quest for a Fantastic Future," page 126.

US$226 million for the company. Tesla was the first to go public since the Motor Ford Company in 1956, a move that paid off well for them. They also opted for a partnership with Toyota to double their effort of developing electric parts, vehicles, along with engineering and support. Their joined forces were to focus on an electrical version for the RAV4 SUV, which Toyota produced.

In 2013, Tesla Motors repaid the loan to the USDE completely, becoming the first car company to have done so while Nissan, Ford, and Fisker were still owing the government money. However, they had problems with their new Model S, which would go on to become "the most loved vehicle in America," according to a 2014 survey. Three of those had issues with the battery, which was very prone to getting damaged if the car struck significant debris. Also, a Model S car caught fire while it was charging at a Supercharger station, raising another problem, though thankfully no one was hurt. As a result of those failures, the Tesla Motors stock fell more than 20 percent. They did fix the issue by creating a battery protection system, which they offered to all models purchased at no cost. And so, the problem was solved without further regulatory action. The drop did not affect Tesla Motors as bad as it could, and they managed to be one of the top performers on the Nasdaq index for the year of 2013.

A Vision for the Future

Tesla Motors wished to spread its influence worldwide, wishing to sell over 33,000 units, and they added to their shipment countries Japan, China, Hong Kong, and Australia. By 2015, Tesla began negotiating with the Chinese government the possibility of producing cars domestically. Their argument was that local production would reduce the sales price by a third in the respective country, as long as there was a demand for it. Musk clarified that the production would remain on American soil; only a factory would be built in places with high-enough demand for the Tesla Model 3, starting with China and possibly expanding to Europe, as well as India, in order to avoid 100 percent import duty.

In late 2014, The Tesla model D, which stands for "dual motor," was unveiled. The car had one motor in the back and one in the front, a sedan that went from 0 to 60 in 3.2 seconds. During the reveal, Musk exclaimed, "This car is nuts. It's like taking off from a carrier deck. It's just bananas. It's like having your own personal roller coaster."[122] Eberhard was invited to attend the event but refused, no longer being on speaking terms with Musk.

In 2015, they produced a record of 13,091 vehicles for both models available, and they also had a high demand for the Model 3, which was to be "unveiled" in March 2016, after being postponed and delayed a couple of times. Only a week after the official reveal, worldwide reservations totaled 325,000 units. As a result of such high demand, Tesla Motors advanced its 500,000 annual unit build plan to include 2018. The human resources vice president, Amnon Geshuri, had a vision to "bring back to California" manufacturing jobs. He announced that they had an amazing surge in hiring's, with 1.5 million worldwide applications in a matter of fourteen months. Geshuri was sure that was a sign that "people want to work here." He also pinpointed the need of hiring veterans as they are "a great source of talent for Tesla."

Still in 2015, Tesla Motors signed a production contract with Group Lotus, a British automotive company specialized in race cars and sports cars and their old contact and reliable partner. They wanted Tesla to produce gliders for them. Gliders are vehicles that do not have a powertrain, especially an engine. They are usually used as a base to create novel or exotic variations of existing vehicles. The contract was available until March 2011, when it was prolonged and refocused of the production of electric Roadsters, which led to a sale of 2,400 units up to December that year. In that period, Tesla also sold zero-emission vehicles to Honda and other automakers. Also, the Model S got an update after allegations that the car's entertainment system could be used as an entryway for hackers.

In August 2016, Tesla purchased Solar City Corp., the largest installer of rooftop solar systems in the United States, for $2.6 billion in stock. After the acquisition was approved, Tesla changed the sales tactics from the door-to-door approach to marketing the solar systems at com-

---

[122] Drake Baer (2014), "The Making of Tesla: Invention, Betrayal, and the Birth of the Roadster," *Business Insider.*

pany showrooms. As a downside, Tesla does not provide a leasing option for the solar panels—the customers have to purchase them.

The year 2016 was also the year when a Tesla car on autopilot mode crashed, leading to the death of its pilot. This is considered to be the first accident with a Tesla car that resulted in the demise of the owner. After an investigation, the conclusion was that "a safety-related defect trend has not been identified at this time, and further examination of this issue does not appear to be warranted," absolving Tesla of all blame.

Besides the crash, Tesla also re-encountered the hacking issue, when researchers at Tencent's Keen Security Lab demonstrated how the car can be controlled without any physical contact. The remote control could guide the car both in driving and parking mode, showing how vulnerable the vehicle was. They managed to "crack" the car by using its web browser while the vehicle was connected to a malicious Wi-Fi. Tesla fixed the issue in a matter of days before the problem was even made public.

The Good and Bad of 2017

At the beginning of 2017, Tesla Motors became Tesla, Inc. The year was a stellar one for the company. In March, Tencent Holdings Ltd., China's golden company at that time, purchased a 5 percent stake in the company at the price of $1.8 billion. The Tesla surpassed GM and Ford as the most valuable automaker (in market capitalization) for a couple of months. And in June that year, they finally made it on the Fortune 500 list—a list that ranks corporations by total revenue. It ranked at 383 by having a revenue increase of 73 percent.

But in July of 2017, Tesla's stock market value decreased again. The investors were disappointed that the demand for the other two models, which were more luxurious, was not growing. It seemed like the introduction of the Model 3 was damaging the sales of the other two, and the fact that customer deposits for them fell by $50 million seemed to prove that theory. They believed it was a case of the Osborne effect. The discussion of the upcoming Model 3 had a negative effect on the sale of the other models, which was no good since the new sedan was on the cheaper side of the price axis. Concerns were so bad that Jeff

Osborne, an analyst, affirmed that "either the Model 3 will cannibalize Model S sales or that customers who reserved the Model 3 may be disappointed when the final product is not a cheaper, next iteration of the Model S."

Investors were also concerned about the future of Tesla since new competitors were ready to put them to the test. Volvo Cars announced that by 2019 it looked forward to introducing only electric or hybrid cars. The market was about to get crowded.

The company had troubles with building battery packs for their cars, and Model 3 was no exception. The production of their latest model was still "a huge challenge" for Tesla, reducing their prediction from 100,000 units to 220, which was "less than anticipated due to production bottlenecks." In November 2017, Musk let the investors know about a production delay, which they needed in order to solve the issues with the new battery that could reduce the manufacturing cost of the Model 3. The robots on the assembly line had issues cause by "systems integration subcontractor." According to Musk, the only thing that solved the problems was to "rewrite all of the software from scratch for the battery module." Elon assured investors that he had engineers working on the issues, but by that time, the director of battery engineering, Jon Wagner, had already left the company. More delays were announced to the frustration of the investors, which reported that "Elon Musk needs to stop overpromising and underdelivering." The production of Model 3 lost the company more money than they ever dared to expect.

A Bad Move

The year of 2018 came with taking privatization into consideration. Musk believed that Tesla's public status put a lot of pressure on the decision-making process regarding every quarter, which could instead affect the company on long-term growth. He also thought that investors had the perfect opportunity to attack the company since it had the shortest stock on the history of the stock market.

"In my opinion, the value of Tesla will rise considerably in the coming months and years, possibly putting any take-private beyond the reach of any investors. It was now or perhaps never," Musk said.[123]

He did clarify eventually that all those arguments were only his personal opinion and not the official one as a CEO of Tesla. On August 18, Musk presented a plan for Tesla's privatization, and most members of his board were supportive of the idea. Some members did not like his "openness" toward social media confessions, and he did promise to better control himself in the future. Advisors started popping up, and a list of possible investors for the privatization plan was made.

Despite having a good privatization offer from Saudi's sovereign wealth fund, on August 24, he announced that the company will keep its public status. He took that decision mostly because he had too many reserves. He feared that rivals could take a stake in Tesla, and he did not like the idea that some of Tesla's loyal supporters could be taken aback by the privatization of the company. When the financial advisors of Tesla said that the privatization of the firm could be done, he simply replied, "Based on the latest information I have, I'm withdrawing the proposal."[124]

In September 2018, Musk felt the heat caused by his publicized opinion. The US Security and Exchange Commission sued him for making misleading and damaging statements.

Musk made a statement after the SEC press conference: "This unjustified action by the SEC leaves me deeply saddened and disappointed. I have always taken action in the best interests of truth, transparency, and investors. Integrity is the most important value in my life, and the facts will show I never compromised this in any way."[125]

Elon Musk settled with them but was forced to step down as a chairman, as well as being prohibited to run for chairman position for another three years, and both he and Tesla were fined with a $20 million fee to reimburse damaged investors. He admitted that the settlement was "fair and reasonable" despite calling them the "Shortseller Enrich-

---

[123] Simon Alvarez (2018), "How Elon Musk Walked Away from Tesla's Privatization despite $30 Billion Offer," *TESLARATI.*

[124] Simon Alvarez (2018), "How Elon Musk Walked Away from Tesla's Privatization despite $30 Billion Offer," *TESLARATI.*

[125] Sasha Lekach (2018), "Elon Musk Tweeted about Taking Tesla Private—Now the SEC Is Suing Him," *Mashable.*

ment Commission" on Twitter. In an interview, he went on to further express that he "has no respect for the SEC." After Musk resigned his post as a chairman, he was replaced by Robyn Denholm.

The year 2018 came with another problem as two teenagers had died after crashing a Tesla Model S into a wall while driving at an illegal speed. According to the parents of the driver Barrett Riley, the young man had a history of overspending, so they had a limiter installed to prevent him from going over 85 mph. But during a service visit, the limiter was taken out without the parents' knowledge, which ultimately allows him to indulge in over speeding again. The removal of the limiter, along with the supposition that the battery was faulty, makes up the base of a lawsuit against Tesla that was filed at the beginning of 2019.

Following one of Musk's tweets that claimed that Tesla would build half a million cars in 2019, the SEO filed another suit against him for violating the terms of the settlement. Musk replied in his usual fashion via Twitter: "SEC forgot to read Tesla earnings transcript, which clearly states 350K to 500K. How embarrassing." Elon's recklessness in his public responses allegedly led to the resignation of Dane Butswinkas, Tesla's general counsel.

A Bright Future for Tesla

Thanks to Model 3's success, Tesla's stock skyrocketed in October. Citroen said that while "the media has been focused on Elon Musk's eccentric, outlandish, and at times offensive behavior, it has failed to notice the legitimate disruption of the auto industry that is currently being *dominated* by Tesla."[126] Perhaps they were right—Musk is really a peculiar character, and it's easy to lose sight of his enterprises. Tesla was going strong, "destroying the competition" at the time when media waited for Musk's next wrong move.

At the end of 2018, Tesla finally managed to outsell Mercedes-Benz in the US market. Also, it reached number 280 on the Fortune 500 list, making "the biggest leap" of that year as a result of the Model S and Model X sales.

---

[126] Claudia Assis (2018), "Tesla Stock Skyrockets after Legendary Short Seller Goes Long," *MarketWatch*.

Tesla has stores, service centers, supercharge stations, and destination charging spots all around the world from the United States to Canada, Mexico, China, Japan, Europe, and others.

As of 2019, Tesla has four factories:

1. The Tesla Factory in Fremont, California—the site was considered dead before Tesla took it under their possession. Modifications were made to the former New United Motor Manufacturing so it could sustain the development and manufacturing of electric cars.

2. Gigafactory 1 in Storey County, Nevada—it's the factory where they first started to produce their lithium-ion batteries. It is aligned on true north so the equipment such as GPS and solar panels could be properly aligned.

3. Gigafactory 2 in Buffalo, New York, which is operated by the SolarCity unit.

4. Gigafactory 3 in Shanghai, China—the unveiling ceremony was held on January 2019, and it's Tesla's first step toward producing cars outside of the United States.

During his visit to China, Musk met the Chinese premier Li Keqiang, who was said to offer Musk "a green card" as to make it easier for him to visit after Elon confessed his love for the country.

Tesla is looking to build a big European factory, either in Germany or the Netherlands.

There are many planned vehicles for the future, such as a Tesla semi-trailer truck, a Model Y, a full-sized SUV designed for families, a Tesla Minibus, and a cheaper car than the Model 3. Regarding the last one, Musk said in a conference in 2016, "There will be future cars that will be even more affordable down the road . . . With fourth-generation and smaller cars and whatnot, we'll ultimately be in a position where everyone can afford the car."

It's quite clear that Tesla wants to make electric cars the primary type of vehicle on the road by tweaking the specifications of their products to make them as close to perfection as possible while also trying to stick to an inclusive price range. This method is very similar to Elon

Musk's approach to space traveling, with the focus being on affordability and quality. The goal is also similar to that of SpaceX, protecting the environment and creating a more inclusive market for eco-friendly products.

Now that the Y model has been officially announced as of 2019, Musk is very happy that Tesla's line of cars put together spells "S 3 X Y," meaning *sexy*. It looks as if this was his plan all along, especially since the Model 3 was supposed to be named Model E and the 3 was used as a substitute (especially in text messages the number 3 often replaces the letter *e*). Musk's jokes are sometimes on a whole different level, adding to his charismatic personality or weirdness, as some call it.

Powerwall and Powerpack

In 2012, Tesla started to develop energy storage products that were meant to be for home use. The Powerwall and the Powerpack are rechargeable lithium-ion battery storage products that mainly use solar energy. As a result, they reduce the electrical bill by a whopping 20 percent.

The Powerwall

It's one of the first small-scale batteries designed for home energy storage on the market. The first version of the Powerwall launched in 2015, after a long testing period where about five hundred pilot units were installed, and in 2016 it got an update. The Powerwall best works with a system of solar panels, which Tesla can provide through their Solar City branch.

Regarding prices, the storage product is quite a hefty investment. Customers pay for the unit, the hardware, its installation, taxes, and many other knickknacks, which could raise the price bar up to $16,000 in the worst case scenario. On the long run, though, most agree that it is worth it.

The battery is designed to work daily and with the help of a solar panel system. When the solar panels produce extra energy that's not required for the day-to-day energy consumption of your house, the Powerwall comes in and stores that energy for later use. In this way, you achieve a balance between production and consumption of energy. However, the Powerwall will only provide energy for a few hours, so depending only on your alternative energy source is not the best idea as of right now. It's more of a way to make your house more cost-efficient.

With time and after constant use, the battery will slowly lose some of its ability to charge. That happens to all batteries, and it does not come as a sign of faulty design. Tesla offers a ten-year warranty and a guarantee that the battery will maintain about 70 percent of its capacity, which is as much as you can ask from a small residential storage product.

The Powerpack

While the Powerwall is a small-scale product, the Powerpack is a bigger unit that comes with both commercial and utility use. According to Musk, "Powerpack is infinitely scalable" in order to meet demands. It contains sixteen individual battery pods, each with their own converters.

The Powerpack is controlled by intelligent software, an on-site computer, and it's fully integrated into your house system. It's designed to be safe by having low-voltage batteries along with a converter, and it comes with a system that cools or heats liquids to ensure its thermal safety and maximum performance.

It helps with cutting the bills' costs down by discharging when the demand for energy is high and by shifting energy consumption from one point to another. The discharge-and-recharge process happens in conformity to a demand signal to ensure peak performance at all times. Also, in emergency situations, the Powerpack provides backup energy to both on-site and off-site locations to eliminate the need to upgrade old infrastructures.

The Powerpack is made as an answer to the rising need for energy storage products. It's a versatile product that can meet high demands no matter the weather conditions. It is an important piece in Tesla's wish to change the way that the world uses energy, "fostering a clean energy ecosystem and helping wean the world off fossil fuels."

Model S

The Model S is an electric five-door lift-back car designed to allow great amounts of impact protection. It puts safety—thanks to its structure and its advanced autopilot functions—and performance at its top priorities. It holds the world record for the fastest acceleration, going from 0 to 60 in 2.4 seconds. The Model S has a wide range of 335 miles and plenty of recharge points all around the world—all of those being Tesla's personal Supercharger stations, which allow for a fast charge. It's made to accommodate five adults, and it also sports outstanding sounds dynamics that can easily compete with a recording studio.

In 2013, it became the first electric car to top the new car sales ranking in any country, with the United States being its leading market. It was also the top-selling plug-in electric car worldwide for the year 2015 as well as 2016. Model S made it on the best 25 inventions of the year 2012—a list created by *Time* magazine.

Also, it won the following:

- World Green Car of the Year (2013)
- Motor Trend Car of the Year (2013)
- Car of the Year 2013 (chosen by the *Automobile* magazine)
- Car of the Century (2015, chosen by *Car and Driver*)
- Top scoring in road testing (Consumers Reports)

An early version (from 2008) of the Model S was designed to include a gasoline engine to extend its driving range, but Elon Musk decided that Tesla will only produce fully electric cars. The production started in 2010 at the Tesla Factory in Fremont California.

Model S came with many new features or even never-before-seen ones in the car manufacturing industry. Its body is made from aluminum, which is very hard to work with as it can tear when pressed, and the paint does not adhere as well compared to other materials. A good example of something that Tesla pioneered was the touch screen. Musk told Ashlee Vance the challenges that it brought: "When we first talked about the touch screen, the guys came back and said,

'There's nothing like that in the automotive supply chain.' I said, 'I know. That's because it's never been put in a fucking car before.'"[127] The touch screen ended up causing Tesla engineers a major headache. They considered laptop screens as a base, but all the manufacturers kept telling them that the laptops were not made to resist in driving conditions. Musk pressed for actual testing to see if they would be able to sustain the temperature fluctuations, and to everybody's surprise, they did. "I'm pretty sure that we ended up with the only seventeen-inch touch screen in the world. None of the computer makers or Apple had made it work yet," Musk added.[128]

It classifies both as a luxury car and a sports car. Because it was designed to be exclusively electric, it comes with a set of special features that make it stand out from the car, such as a front and a rear trunk and an enlarged front crumple zone.

A study conducted by the University of California came in 2016 to the conclusion that "environmental, performance, and technological motivations are reasons for adoption; the new technology brings a new segment of buyers into the market; and financial purchase incentives are not important in the consumer's decision to adopt a high-end BEV," summing up that electric cars, such as the Model S, are the future of auto vehicles.

Model X

The Model X is Tesla's "safest SUV ever," its strong structure making it very improbable for the passengers to sustain any sort of injury in terms of frontal and side impact crashes.

It was developed from the full-sized platform of the Model S, and it combines luxury with utility. It has room for seven people, and it sports comfortable seating, along with a capacity to tow up to 5,000 pounds. The doors have a special opening mechanism called the Falcon Wing Doors, which can open even in the tightest of parking spots.

---

[127] Ashlee Vance (2015), "Elon Musk: Tesla, SpaceX, and the Quest for a Fantastic Future," pages 163–164.

[128] Ashlee Vance (2015), "Elon Musk: Tesla, SpaceX, and the Quest for a Fantastic Future," page 164.

It has a slightly smaller range than the S Model, with only 295 miles, which is still a lot for an electric car, and it has plenty of Supercharger stations where it can be charged in no time, as to not disturb the driver's road experience. The systems of the Model X respond quicker than you would expect a bulky car to, with an acceleration that can take you from 0 to 60 in 2.8 seconds. It has a spoiler to provide aerodynamics and a low drag coefficient, making it rise above other vehicles from its class.

Deliveries began in 2015 after a series of delays caused by issues with the cooling system of the motor and with the door opening mechanism.

Awards:

- 2016 Reader's Choice Green Car of the Year and Luxury Utility Vehicle of the Year
- The Golden Steering Wheel in the Large SUV category
- Top Green Vehicle Overall in the SUV/Minivan category (by the American Automobile Association)
- The Australian Good Design Award in the Automotive and transport category for its "athletic build"
- Forbes Best Vehicle of the Year (2017)

It also achieved a world record for the heaviest tow made by an electric production passenger vehicle by pulling a Boeing 787 almost 1,000 feet.

Although it's an award-winning car with many appealing features, it was not met with the same enthusiasm as the Model S. Consumers Report underlined the issues with the doors and the unfoldable second row of seats, going as far as calling the Model X a "firm and choppy ride."

But overall, the large SUV did well for itself, gaining good reviews even from Jeremy Clarkson, a journalist who had brutally criticized Tesla's Roadster in the past—so badly that it caused a lawsuit.

Overall, people liked this bulky but "fabulous" car with unmatched performance and efficiency in its category.

Model 3

The Model 3 is the most affordable car made by Tesla without compromising the quality of their products. It boasts safety above all, with a structure that allows maximum strength in all the car's areas. It goes from 0 to 60 in 3.2 seconds, and it comes with a carbon fiber spoiler to give it more stability at high speeds.

It has two separate motors that allow for better handling and traction control. Also, the car can ride on only one motor if one stops working for any reason, making it less likely to get stuck on the side of the road. It has a range of 178 miles, and it can be charged at home or along the way at Tesla's Supercharger stations. A special feature of this vehicle is that it can use your smartphone as its key.

In its original design, it was considered to be a family car, and it was supposed to be named Model E, which was abandoned due to Ford's trademark. In 2013, Franz von Holzhausen, Tesla's design chief, described the Model 3 as "an Audi A4, BMW 3 Series, Mercedes-Benz C-Class type of vehicle that will offer everything: range, affordability, and performance." The Model was unveiled in 2016, getting over 200,000 order in a span of a few days, a lot of the reservations coming from new Tesla customers.

Production and development were delayed due to unforeseen issues. In 2018, years after its unveiling, it was still not perfect, having a long stopping distance for the emergency brakes system. Tesla manned up and quickly solved that by updating the anti-lock braking company, a fix that made the car become a widely recommended vehicle.

As of 2019, customers are still encountering problems with the car, such as defects and loose body parts. Tesla is working relentlessly to bring the vehicle to premium quality without chipping away at its "affordable" status.

Tesla Autopilot

Although all of Tesla's vehicles have a built-in "self-driving hardware," the company labels the feature as optional, the driver being able to switch it on and off at his will. Their autopilot has two levels:

1. Enhanced autopilot—according to Tesla, it "should still be considered a driver's assistance feature with the driver responsible for remaining in control of the car at all times." The software is bought separately and, based on a the laws of the country in which you're driving it, could allow for a couple of features, such as "match speed to traffic conditions, keep within a lane, automatically change lanes without requiring driver input, transition from one freeway to another, exit the freeway when your destination is near, self-park when near a parking spot, and be summoned to and from your garage," Tesla claims.

2. Full self-driving software—this system is not yet available, but it promises big things, like the car being able to drive short or long distances without any input from the driver. This additional level will come at a separate price, and as for now, Tesla remains ambiguous about it by saying, "It is not possible to know exactly when each element of the functionality described above will be available."

For now, Tesla Autopilot should be seen as a system that makes the drive experience easier but nonetheless requires active input from the driver. It sports useful features like maintaining a safe distance from the vehicle in front of your car, keeping the car between the road's lane marking and also an emergency braking system to minimalize collision risks. However, it requires the driver to pay attention to the road at all times, so Tesla Autopilot is far from being an autonomous or self-driving system, and it should not be treated as such. For example, if the driver chooses to not keep his hands on the steering wheel, the system deploys a message for them to do so and triggers an alarm if no action is taken. If the driver still fails to respond, the car will slowly decelerate until it stops and automatically switches on the warning lights. That's the power of the Tesla Autopilot.

About their system, Tesla declared, "Tesla Autopilot does not prevent all accidents, such a standard would be impossible, but it makes them much less likely to occur. It unequivocally makes the world safer for the vehicle occupants, pedestrians, and cyclists."

On March 23, 2018, a Tesla Model X smashed into a concrete divider, an accident that became the second instance where a driver died in a

Tesla vehicle. To make matters worse, it was revealed that the car had its autopilot on, which in the eyes of the media meant that Tesla was fully responsible. An investigation started, and about a week after the incident, Tesla made its statement on a blog post: "In the moments before the collision, which occurred at 9:27 a.m. on Friday, March 23rd, Autopilot was engaged with the adaptive cruise control follow-distance set to minimum. The driver had received several visual and one audible hands-on warning earlier in the drive, and the driver's hands were not detected on the wheel for six seconds prior to the collision. The driver had about five seconds and 150 meters of unobstructed view of the concrete divider with the crushed crash attenuator, but the vehicle logs show that no action was taken," basically declaring that their system worked as intended and that it did everything it could to stop the accident from happening.

Even before Tesla explained the situation, Waymo boss John Krafcik stepped in to defend the electric car company: "Tesla has driver-assist technology, and that's very different from our approach. If there's an accident in a Tesla, the human in the driver's seat is ultimately responsible for paying attention. We don't know what happened here, but there was no self-driving."[129] Waymo is a self-driving technology development company that strives to offer a fully automated car with a driverless system to the public. It's only natural for John Krafcik to raise awareness of the difference between driver assistance systems such as the one provided by Tesla and a self-driving system that should, indeed, be at blame if a vehicle crashed while on autonomous mode.

Regardless of public confusion when it comes to their autopilot, Tesla works tirelessly to get on the same level with Waymo and Audi and develop a fully automated vehicle that could act as a "robotic taxi."

Teslaquila

Teslaquila was originally Musk's April Fool's joke for the year 2018. He posted a photo of himself passed up next to a Model 3 and surrounded by bottles of the inexistent beverage. His tweets said, "There are many chapters of bankruptcy and, as critics so rightly pointed out, Tesla has

---

[129] Alistair Charlton (2018), "How does Tesla Autopilot works, is it safe, and how does it compare to truly autonomous cars," *Gearbrain.*

them *all*, including Chapter 14 and a half (the worst one). Elon was found passed out against a Tesla Model 3, surrounded by 'Teslaquilla' bottles, the tracks of dried tears still visible on his cheeks. This is not a forward-looking statement, because, obviously, what's the point? Happy New Month!"

What was supposed to be only a joke then cemented itself as a real upcoming Tesla product as Musk trademarked the name and announced it as "coming soon."

Many automakers have a line of merch to get people more involved with the brand even if they might not afford to buy one of their vehicles. So it was only a matter of time until Tesla jumped on the merch wagon by opening up and accessories store. From clothes to Model S toy cars and Starman mugs, the Musk-ian products make a nice profit on their own as there is quite a demand on the market for anything Elon. Why would there not be a demand for something as unique as Tesla-branded booze?

Tequila sales are going good with numbers on the rise as the years go by, and many celebrities have already joined the beverage market by creating and selling their own tequilas—in partnership with already established brands. Although the process of coming up with a unique recipe, labeling, and marketing strategy can be an arduous one, Musk has plenty of resources to invest in the drink, and his influence could put in on the market in a matter of month rather than years.

Mike Morales, the CEO of Tequila Aficionado Media, is quite unsure as to why Musk chose tequila out of all beverages available. "It's a crowded marketplace for a scarce commodity," he said, as a must-have ingredient for tequila is the blue agave, which takes seven years to grow.[130] Not to forget that tequila is a type of drink that has a required "aging time," whereas others (such as vodka, for example) do not. Furthermore, Morales claims that "the industry is in trouble. There's going to be a shakeout. Right now it's a difficult, difficult market."[131] That's because the plant growers have no idea what the demand for the blue agave will be after seven years, and more often than not, producers are not able to keep up with the orders.

---

[130] Elizabeth Lopatto (2018), "Elon Musk's Teslaquila Is Actually a Good Idea," *The Verge*.

[131] Elizabeth Lopatto (2018), "Elon Musk's Teslaquila Is Actually a Good Idea," *The Verge*.

Morales hopes that Musk chose tequila on purpose as to change the industry since it is known for not being exactly "eco-friendly." The filtering process produces a lot of waste, which stirs up another issue. "It's a crisis: where are we going to put the crap when we're done with it?"[132] Morales ponders. Maybe Musk can come up with one of his futuristic ideas to save the planet from the smelly remains?

Public opinions are polarizing. Some believe that it's unwise for car companies to advertise an alcoholic beverage as it may make it seem like it's prompting people to drink and drive. Nora Freeman Engstrom, a law professor, disagrees by affirming, "Unless there's a suggestion (in marketing or otherwise) that the two products should be used together or go hand in hand, I don't see any liability implications."[133] In other words, Tesla is not out there telling people that they promote the idea of drinking while driving their vehicles. The company will just happen to sell two different products at the same time that, when used together, could cause some troubles. With no link between the two except for the Tesla brand, customers should be responsible enough to know better.

Tesla's approach to branching out on its products is quite unique. It's a big leap from apparel and accessories to alcohol, but it does play on the "classy" aspect of Tesla. The company, especially Musk, puts a lot of focus on how their products look and how they make you feel. Their vehicles have an aesthetically pleasing design with a very high comfort factor. Tequila is one of the finer drinks available out there that are very appreciated by the public. So in theory, it should fit well with Tesla's brand. The fact that Teslaquila just happens to sound like a match made in heaven is a bonus.

---

[132] Elizabeth Lopatto (2018), "Elon Musk's Teslaquila Is Actually a Good Idea," *The Verge.*
[133] Elizabeth Lopatto (2018), "Elon Musk's Teslaquila Is Actually a Good Idea," *The Verge.*

Chapter 6: Solar City

Musk was linked to Solar City way before it merged with his big company Tesla. He was the one that gave Lyndon and Peter Rive the suggestion to try their luck in the solar energy market, and he was also one of the first investors, putting about $10 million in the start-up.

Pretorian Stubbornness

The Rive brothers were keen entrepreneurs with the experience of a past software company. They knew how to approach their new enterprise as to keep costs down. That's how Solar City was born, a business with the high goal of promoting alternative energy. They were involved in every step of the experience, from the sale to the installation of the solar panels that were provided by third-party manufacturers.

At first, they only had 150 employees, which were predominantly construction workers, and they did well for themselves, with more than seventy solar panel installations in the span of a year. One of the biggest problems that they had to overcome was the price of the whole system, which was in the field of $40,000. Customers could not afford to buy them, so the brothers thought about a leasing option. They were not the first company to take such a strategy into consideration, and banks were not happy with the idea. The Rive brothers, however, were stubborn Pretorians like another certain someone that supported their business decisions. After a lot of "hammering," they scored an agreement that allowed them to offer solar systems to customers without a down payment. Solar City was able to profit from this strategy because they could claim a 30 percent federal solar tax credit for every installation that they did. The terms of the agreement were as follows:

1. Solar City paid for rooftop designs, panels, installation, and consultations by working with banks to front the capital.

2. Customers had a lease of twenty years in which they paid back Solar City. This was done via monthly payments that were kept at a lower cost than a utility bill.

From a business that was initially a Northern California exclusive, Solar City quickly expanded to more than a dozen states. Even if Musk was not involved in the business past the board level, the brothers shared his ambition and confidence. At the end of 2012, the company went public on the stock market, which led to their sales doubling in numbers with every year that passed. By the beginning of 2014, it had more than 70,000 customers, allowing the Rive brothers to dream of a grand future.

While the company was reaching its goal of making residential solar mainstream, it began having internal issues. As two executives gained more influence, blood started to boil. Tanguy Serra and Hayes Barnard had different visions of Solar City, and they brought their feud to the office. The focus was slightly but surely shifting on the number of sales the company made rather than the change they were bringing to the world, yet the firm made a couple of investments that allowed them to reduce some cost and put more personality into their product. Serra orchestrated the acquisition of Zep Solar, a start-up that developed a mounting system that sped up the installation process considerably from days to a couple of hours. Also, Serra backed by Lyndon acquired Silevo, a solar panel technology business. Silevo was not the best move. The purchase ate up a lot of the firm's capital, close to $200 million, at a time when solar panel prices were dropping.

A Shadow on the Sun

Solar City had its bad moment too. In 2015, at a sales-team huddle in Las Vegas, Chief Revenue Officer Barnard put on quite a show by jumping on stage and rapping over a Nicki Minaj song while scantily dressed women danced around him. He made another appearance dressed as the Greek sun god Helios to further the weirdness factor. It was too much, but the attendees and the performers enjoyed it. Solar City did have reason to celebrate after all. The firm was the industry's leader. It stayed on top by aggressively targeting customers and emphasizing the benefits of its lease deal.

Even so, they had to hire a substantial number of sales representatives in order to keep up, and the majority of them were poorly trained. They did not know how to explain the terms of the lease or what it consisted of. It was more of a "just sign here" kind of thing, and the customers were not happy. Cancellations became a real issue, with a staggering rate of over 45 percent or even 70 percent for the door-to-door teams. Competitors were starting to get a strong grasp on the market, and Solar City's profitability was affected.

The finances of Solar City started looking grim, and it became somewhat dependent on investors. A source confesses, "The reality of solar financing was that most of the cash started coming from investors like Google months after installation. We started having huge gaps in cash flow as the business grew."[134] Its stock value went down.

Lyndon Rive was under pressure. State policies were changing, some even voting to cut benefits from homeowners that had solar installations. That affected Solar City more than expected, and they had to completely pull out of Nevada after such a vote. The federal solar tax credit was not doing any better. Even when that was extended, sales went down as customers realized that they had more time to benefit from the subsidy. Solar City changed its approach by focusing on profitability first and leaving expansion for later. Lyndon admitted that it was time to reduce the growth, and investors liked the sound of that.

In 2016, the sock value dropped even more. They changed the strategy from leasing solar systems to selling them through loans to lower debt and generate interest. Solar City waved goodbye to their trusty monthly payments. Analysts were confused by the firm's shift in strategy, and Serra did not manage to clear the waters during an earnings call. In February that year, Musk got involved, and he proposed a merge between Tesla and Solar City.

Musk and Solar City

The spring before that, Musk announced the Powerwall, a battery storage product that would shift the way people use energy. But production and installations were a mess. Tesla could not even go and make the

---

[134] Austin Carr (2017), "The Real Story Behind Elon Musk's $2.6 Billion Acquisition of Solar City and What It Means for Tesla's Future–Not to Mention the Planet's," *Fast Company*.

98

installation themselves, so customers had to rely on independent installers. If the customers wanted Powerwall linked to a solar source, they again had to get in touch with a different firm, such as Solar City. Musk quickly realized how flawed this system was. He wanted control, and by acquiring Solar City, he would get it. Later on, he confessed that the merger could and should have been done earlier, but Tesla at that time simply had too much going on for it.

The offer from February was not a formal one—both sides wanted to think it through before jumping into it. Musk presented the idea to the Tesla board, and they were not elated with it. The capital was already drained by the development and production of the Model X, so they decided against it at first. In May, when he believed that the issues were solved, he brought the proposal again, unbeknown to anyone at Solar City, including the Rive brothers.

On June, an offer was made—$2.8 billion. Because there were conflicts of interests, Tesla had to express its intentions in a public manner before the offer could be taken into consideration by Solar City. Investors were skeptical. Solar City's financial partners were confused, and they chose to freeze its capital, greatly worsening its already wobbly financial status. A *Wall Street Journal* columnist wrote at the time that "Tesla latching on to Solar City is the equivalent of a shipwrecked man clinging to a piece of driftwood grabbing on to another man without one." No one believed that the merger would bring Tesla any benefits.

In hopes of persuading shareholders and analysts alike, Musk teased a new Solar City product, a solar roof that "looks way better than a normal roof? That lasts far longer than a normal roof? Different ball game." The roof sounded good, but it had a long way to go before it could be considered ready. The prototype received the code name Steel Pulse, and when he laid eyes on it, Musk hated it on an instant. He liked the idea but not what they had done with it. Musk pushed them to a more aesthetically pleasing version, with glass tiles. The joined forces of Tesla and Solar City created a display-worthy demo in a matter of weeks. The merger was approved in November.

Solar City now had plans for a new manufacturing plant in Buffalo, to the happiness of the locals. They saw it as an opportunity for Buffalo to

gain some importance, but it also brought new work-related opportunities. The people understood what Solar City meant as a company—a
hope for the future. A future they wanted to help build. A lot of governmental funding was chopped in order to get the facility on its feet as
soon as possible. Of course, there were delays and budget issues.
They purchased types of machinery that stood still and waited for construction to be done, which seemed to be a distant dream. Solar City
had to confirm that production was stalled: "It all just stopped. We were
going to rely on Solar City's money to finish the Buffalo project, but our
sales were so far down that all the money just stopped."[135] Ultimately,
Solar City needed to bring Panasonic, an outsider partner to manage
the final costs and take over cell manufacturing. The factory received
the name Gigafactory 2, and it was raised on a site that Solar City
gained back in 2014 when they purchased Silevo.

All was nice and well in theory, but challenges soon appeared. The aim
was to build high-efficiency solar panels that could convert energy at a
higher percentage, something they started at Silevo, which they hoped
could be done at Buffalo in the future. They had to do that while solar
panel prices were dropping on a global level. There were also problems with the manufacturing process. The merge allowed for Tesla and
Solar City to share both expertise and resources, but Musk was focused on pumping up the production numbers for Model 3, and he did
not even tour the new-built factory.

Despite Tesla's announcements that Solar City was going fine, layoffs
of almost 3,000 people from the sales and marketing departments tell
another story. Serra and Barnard were also long gone, as well as the
CEO of Silevo and the head of Zep Solar. Their installations dropped
significantly, and their model further shifted toward loans. Musk admitted that in the future there will be no Solar City but a new branch
known as Tesla Solar. From the outside, it seemed like Elon Musk
stepped in to save Solar City when its star began to fade, but Lyndon
sees it differently. To him, there was no need for an "Ave Maria" or a
"savior." Solar City could have made it out of the crisis, he believed,
and the significant rise in the "cash flow" before the merger seems to

[135] Austin Carr (2017), "The Real Story Behind Elon Musk's $2.6 Billion Acquisition of Solar City
and What It Means for Tesla's Future–Not to Mention the Planet's," *Fast Company*.

back him up. Regarding Musk's abilities as a CEO, Lyndon confessed that he as a company head can "punch through many walls." But "Elon can punch through every wall. That's the difference between us."[136]

In 2017, Lyndon parted ways with Solar City just a few months after the merger was officially closed. His departure was somewhat unexpected, but he wished to take a break from projects that could have such a big impact on humanity, and he believed that the "vision" behind Solar City could still work without his presence. His brother Peter followed suit in July of the same year.

In August 2017, Tesla began the manufacturing of the Tesla Solar Roofs at the Buffalo factory. After a couple of tests, in 2018, Tesla announced that commercial customers' installations will commence in a matter of months.

Musk remains fixated on his plans to use both Tesla and Solar City as a way to "save" the environment, but he denies having any "god complex," which others bestow on him. He does not want to fit in the role of the "savior." Elon Musk just wants to do his part as well as possible and make a change.

---

[136] Austin Carr (2017), "The Real Story Behind Elon Musk's $2.6 Billion Acquisition of Solar City and What It Means for Tesla's Future–Not to Mention the Planet's," *Fast Company*.

Chapter 7: Hyperloop

Hyperloop is another concept that Elon Musk came up with. He first presented this idea in 2012 after describing how he once destroyed an F1 race car. He said, "Right now we've got planes, trains, automobiles, and boats. But what if there was a fifth mode? I have a name for it: the Hyperloop." Having as a base example Robert Goddard's vactrain high-speed rail transportation, a Hyperloop defines a sealed system of tubes through which a pod may travel free of friction or air resistance. In Musk's idea, this system could allow for a speed of more than 1,000 km/h, revolutionizing the way we see transport today. It would be immune to weather conditions, safer than most ways of transport as it would have a zero chance of collision, twice as fast as a plane, and energy efficient. All that would apply to a means of transportation made to go in a loop. He described the Hyperloop as a "cross between a Concorde and a railgun and an air hockey table."

However, Musk was already busy with both SpaceX and Tesla; he had no time for another life-altering project. So his next move was understandable even if it had some shock to it: he made the idea available for anyone that wanted to give it a try. But he could not stay completely away from the Hyperloop. A group of engineers from the two companies created a conceptual model for the transportation system and published it on the SpaceX and Tesla blogs. The concept included a possible design, the functionality of the system, the pathways, as well as a general cost. The ideal Hyperloop had to be energy-efficient and allow mass transportation. Musk invited people to offer their opinions on the concept in order to improve it. For that, he made the Alpha concept available as an open source design.

In 2015, SpaceX announced that it would start the construction of a test track near its Hawthorne facility to be used by third parties that designed their versions of the pod. The Hyperloop became a project that amassed more interest than Musk could have ever expected. Student teams and firms alike flocked to the idea, seeing the potential behind the concept.

In 2016, a team from the Massachusetts Institute of Technology developed the first ever prototype of the Hyperloop pod. It used electrodynamic suspension to ensure levitation and an eddy current braking, which slows a moving object by transforming its kinetic energy in heat.

In 2017, SpaceX sponsored the first on-track Hyperloop pod competition, which used the test track named the Hypertube to assess the performance of the prototype pods. The judges were engineers from the company, and the results were as follows:

- The team from Delft University had the highest competition score.

- The team from the Technical University of Munich (TUM Hyperloop) had the fastest pod with the best performance in flight.

- The team from the MIT placed third, despite their pod demonstrating the first low-pressure Hyperloop run in the world.

In the next competition that was judged on the pod's top speed along with a successful deceleration, TUM Hyperloop won, managing to break the existent speed record. Their pod could achieve the top speed of 324 km/h.

Since the idea was born, many companies raised to fill in the concept with their own original ideas. Out of those, two names stand out: Hyperloop Transportation Technologies and Virgin Hyperloop One. The competition between the two companies is very intense, each trying to outsmart the other and develop a working product that also adheres to regulations before the other.

But it's not all bad blood between the Hyperloop "lords." Even if they are not directly involved in a partnership, both assured the population that interconnectivity between their respective routes would be possible in order to facilitate commercial transport. After all, a certain level of co-operation is necessary if Hyperloop is to become the fifth mode of transportation. According to Richard Geddes, a professor and a co-founder of the Hyperloop Advanced Research Partnership, "Hyperloop has a number of incredible benefits as a new mode of transport, including energy usage, speed, and safety—and it's not just hype. There's too many smart people working on it and too much capital behind it for it to not be realized."[137]

The big issue is not making the transportation method work but to ensure that it fits safety standards. Many critics of the project believe that the riding experience in itself would be unpleasant. From the narrow space to the windowless pod, high noise levels and turbulence caused by the high speed, Hyperloop does not sound like your typical first-class trip. There are also many questions regarding emergency evacuation plans, malfunctions, and accident risks. With maglev trains, like the Japanese ScMaglev, which achieve remarkable speeds without the need of a tube already on the market, Hyperloop tube-based system is frowned upon. A faulty tube design could cause catastrophic accidents. Professor Richard Muller, an American physicist, also warns about how "[the Hyperloop's] novelty and the vulnerability of its tubes would be a tempting target for terrorists," which is a matter to be taken into consideration.[138]

Even with critics spoiling the party for everybody, there is already talk of possible routes for a Hyperloop system. In the United States, the route proposed links the Greater Los Angeles Area to the San Francisco Bay Area. With those being two major metropolitan areas, the costs for construction would not be that high, but due to the need of other methods of transportation, the total travel time would get longer rather than shortening it. Future plans revolve around constructing a loop between Cleveland and Chicago. At the end of 2018, Musk showed to the public a three-kilometer tunnel below Los Angeles that fit his initial concept that Hyperloops should be built below the ground.

For India, Hyperloop Transportation Technologies already signed a contract to build a route connecting Amaravathi to Vijayawada, making it a six-minute ride. Other possible routes that have been in the talks are Helsinki-Stockholm, Toronto-Montreal, Edinburg-London, Paris-Amsterdam, Seoul-Busan, and many others. The whole world wants to

[137] Anthony Cuthbertson (2018), "Hyperloop: The 1,000 KPH Race to Realize Elon Musk's Improbable Dream Heats Up in the Middle East," *Independent.*
[138] Troy Wolverton (2013), "Elon Musk's Hyperloop hype ignores practical problems," *The Mercury News.*

benefit from this new type of technology available. Following into the steps of the saying "Go big or go home," Musk already envisioned how the Hyperloop could be used on Mars, because according to him, due to the planet's atmosphere, there would be no need for a tube system, only a track.

The Hyperloop project is feasible because it reduces construction costs over conventional passenger rails, and according to Musk, it would also have a minimal impact on the environment, though both of those statements are debatable. Alon Levy, a mass transportation writer, gave his own opinion on the matter: "In reality, an all-elevated system (which is what Musk proposes with the Hyperloop) is a bug rather than a feature. Central Valley land is cheap; pylons are expensive, as can be readily seen by the costs of elevated highways and trains all over the world."[139] Economists and transportation experts alike also came together to the agreement that the cost of the Hyperloop system will highly exceed Musk's expectations. Political and economical environments would also have to be taken into consideration before choosing the areas where such a system could be implemented.

Regardless of setbacks and polarizing opinions, all the players in the Hyperloop designing and manufacturing game are doing their best to bring Musk's idea to life, with intensive trials taking place in deserts or other available areas. People can say what they want about Elon Musk, but they cannot deny his deep involvement in triggering the dawn of a new futuristic era.

---

[139] Brad Plumer (2013), "There is no redeeming feature of the Hyperloop," *The Washington Post.*

Chapter 8: OpenAI

OpenAI is a nonprofit research organization focused on artificial intelligence. The purpose of OpenAI is to develop a friendly artificial intelligence that would end supporting and aiding humanity. The organization was founded by Elon Musk and Sam Atman in 2015, and it aims to start collaborations with other research institutions by making their discoveries and projects open to the public.

In 2016, OpenAI released a public beta of OpenAI Gym. The platform's purpose is to provide a general intelligence benchmark for a variety of environments. It aims to find a standard for how environments are defined by AI in order to make future research easier. In December of the same year, OpenAI released a software platform for training and measuring AI in the field of games, applications, and websites called Universe.

Other products made by OpenAI are as follows:

- RoboSumo—it's a meta-learning program in which two robots that originally lack general knowledge are given the goal to learn how to move around and defeat their adversary. This method admittedly helps agents adapt to new environments and boosts their abilities of learning and functioning.

- OpenAI Five—a team of bots that engage in competitive Dota 2 matches against human players chosen randomly. This idea of man versus AI in the world of Dota2 was initially tried with a one-versus-one match between a bot and a professional player, which resulted in the player losing against the AI. The bot had learned how to play by constantly having matches with itself for two weeks straight. AIs learn over time and are rewarded for achieving different tasks such as "killing" an enemy. By 2018, the team was formed, and it had its first matches against pro teams, both being won by the players. The project is considered to be a success.

- Debate Game—machines learn how to debate toy issues in front of a human judge in order to assist their decision-making process and to develop and explainable AI.

- Dactyl—it trains a robot Shadow Hand using a similar learning algorithm as for the OpenAI Five.

- GPT2—it's a system that generates text to match a tone. Unlike other OpenAI products and project, this has not been released to the public, as it can be used to create and spread false news.

There are many big names that support the OpenAI initiative, from Peter Thiel (PayPal co-founder) to Amazon's Web Services and Reid Hoffman (LinkedIn co-founder).

However, OpenAI pays research salaries that are nowhere near those offered by Facebook or Google. So most of the people working for the organization do it for the future potential that it offers. For example, Ilya Sutskever, who worked as a research scientist at Google Brain, chose to give up his Google career for a post at OpenAI "partly because of the very strong group of people and, to a very large extent, because of its mission."[140]

Even if artificial intelligence could end up helping humanity, there are still risks to developing a potentially superior "being." Many bright minds, the likes of Stephen Hawking and Stuart Russell, fear that it could lead to the extinction of the human race. Musk himself affirmed that AI is one of mankind's "biggest existential threat." He went further by declaring, "I'm increasingly inclined to think that there should be some regulatory oversight, maybe at the national and international level, just to make sure that we don't do something very foolish. With artificial intelligence, we are summoning the demon."[141]

That's why OpenAI tries to develop a friendly system, but they do realize that it's a very delicate balance between the benefits and the

---

[140] Cade Metz (2016), "Inside OpenAI, Elon Musk's Wild Plan to Set Artificial Intelligence Free," *Wired Magazine*.

[141] Samuel Gibbs (2014), "Elon Musk: artificial intelligence is our biggest existential threat," *The Guardian*.

threats that AI could bring to our society. OpenAI's aim is to aid human-ity and prepare for the time when humans are ready to accept autono-mous intelligent machines in their midst. Sam Altman expressed his thought on this issue: "Are we really willing to let our society be infil-trated by autonomous software and hardware agents whose details of operation are known only to a select few? Of course not," admitting that their project is one for the future.[142]

At the start of 2019, Musk declared that he stepped down from OpenAI on amicable terms. He used Twitter to explain his departure from the organization: "I had to focus on solving a painfully large number of en-gineering & manufacturing problems at Tesla (especially) & SpaceX. Also, Tesla was competing for some of same people as OpenAI & I didn't agree with some of what OpenAI team wanted to do. Add that all up & it was just better to part ways on good terms." In other words, it is the tight schedule and differences of interest that caused the rift and not internal issues.

Nevertheless, his involvement with the nonprofit organizations comes once again to show that Elon Musk's goal is to create a better future for mankind in any way possible, regardless of the monetary gain that comes out of his enterprises.

---

[142] Glen W.Smith (2018), "Re: Sex–Bots—Let Us Look before We Leap."

Chapter 9: Neuralink

Neuralink is a neuro-technology company founded by Musk and many others. It strives to develop interfaces to connect human brains with computers.

On a Joe Rogan podcast, he explained the idea behind Neuralink in a simple, understandable way: "How much smarter are you with a phone or computer or without? You're vastly smarter, actually. You can answer any question pretty much instantly. You can remember flawlessly. Your phone can remember videos [and] pictures perfectly. Your phone is already an extension of you. You're already a cyborg. Most people don't realize you're already a cyborg. It's just that the data rate . . . It's slow, very slow. It's like a tiny straw of information flow between your biological self and your digital self. We need to make that tiny straw like a giant river, a huge, high-bandwidth interface."

The Neuralink project follows the same pattern as Musk's other initiatives—a futuristic concept designed to improve our lives and get humanity one step closer to a scientific revolution. Besides the focus on enhancing the abilities of the human mind, Neuralink also strives to create devices that could treat brain injuries. The long-term goal of the company is to "achieve symbiosis with artificial intelligence" via implants, or as Musk put it, to "effectively merge with AI."

In 2018, records show that Neuralink wishes to open an animal testing facility in San Francisco and started a round of research at the University of California, Davis. The company keeps its projects private.

Only the future will tell what Neuralink will achieve and if it will rise up to Musk's sci-fi-ish aspirations.

Chapter 10: The Boring Company

Musk has already previously shown his interest in transforming the way people commute with his ambitious Hyperloop idea. But at the end of 2016, he decided to take on an active role by founding the Boring Company, an infrastructure and tunnel construction enterprise. Like most of his decisions, he announced this on Twitter in his usual jokey manner: "Traffic is driving me nuts. Am going to build a tunnel boring machine and just start digging." This was followed by a serious "I am actually going to do this." And so the Boring Company was born, and the rest is history. It was initially a subsidiary of SpaceX until 2018, when it became independent.

From the outside, it seems like the billionaire has a strange liking for tunnels, which he explains with logical solid arguments like they don't change much the infrastructure of a city, as they are underground. They are a long-time construction. They allow for high-speed transport. They connect cities, and of course, they have a sci-fi look to them. Elon Musk is known to swoon over any futuristic-looking machine that promises life-altering changes for the better.

Also, for Musk, the Boring Company is the firm that lets his imagination run wild. They have a mascot Gary, a snail that is a real version of SpongeBob's pet, which even has a pineapple habitat. And they let him go on with his quirky merchandise ideas, such as lego-type construction kits and flamethrowers—more on those later.

Tunnels are a pretty mundane thing that humankind has already mastered as a structure, or so we believe. Sure, the tunnels made now are better than those constructed in 1843, the year in which the first tunnel became available to the public. The Boring Company comes in to teach us not how to build underground structures but how to do it in a more efficient and cost-effective manner while also rushing the digging process—all that without compromising the quality of the overall construction.

To make those improvements, the Boring Company uses its new "boring" assets:

- Support strategies—the company wishes to find a way in which they can both dig and secure the tunnels at the same time.

- Tunnel machines—their actual machines go slow and steady, but they get the job done. The newest one has three times the power and operates with electricity

- Redesigning tunnels—the Boring Company believes that smaller is better in this situation, going for structures that are half the size of modern tunnels, making them cheaper.

- Looking for new methods and technologies for tunneling— something that most people did not see as necessary and that will highly speed up the process.

There are many things to take into consideration besides the actual building process. The Boring Company needs to make sure that critical conditions, such as earthquakes, would not affect the integrity of the tunnels. To make sure the structures will hold when confronted with massive vibrations, the tunnels are deep underground. To solve the emissions problems, the tunneling equipment can't be fully electric, at least not yet. The company opted for an electric skate method, which proved effective. The Boring Company also managed to come up with ways to recycle dirt to make the process even more cost-efficient.

There was another issue created by their approach, and that was designing cars or other transportation methods that could fit in the small tunnels. The company came up with some possible ideas, but some people worry that the tunnels will only be compatible with the firm's vehicles. In July 2017, Elon Musk uploaded a video showing a successful test performed with a prototype car elevator.

These are the names of the three actual "boring machines":

1. Gadot, named after the Becket play *Waiting for Godot*

2. Line-Storm, which took its name from "A Line-Storm Song," one of Robert Frost's poems

3. Prufrock, named after T. S. Eliot's first professionally published poem, "The Love Song of J. Alfred Prufrock"

Musk loves to give all his creations names with hidden meaning or that pay homage to some of his favorite songs, literary works, or movies.

As of projects, the Boring Company has built a test tunnel that was unveiled to the public in 2018. Musk remembered how their first test started with a big letdown when his employees told him on a Friday that it would take two weeks just to move their cars in the parking lot available. To which Musk responded, "Let's get started today and see what the biggest hole we can dig is between now and Sunday afternoon, running twenty-four hours a day."[143] A response that prompted them to get the job done in record time.

The Boring Company has proposed many future constructions that are yet to be approved—one to link parts of Los Angeles with the Dodger Stadium, one to connect downtown Chicago to the O'Hare Airport, and a bolder one that would create a connection between Baltimore and Washington, DC. It remains to be seen whatever project will actually become a reality.

One project, though, seems like it's not meant to be. New York City officials reached out to the Boring Company with an idea of connecting Times Square with the John F. Kennedy International Airport, but engineers found more than one obstacle that makes the installation of a loop system highly improbable. There are worries regarding the city's infrastructure, mainly that it would not be compatible with Musk's tunnels. The bad ventilation system poses a big threat, as it has always for public transportation in NYC. And last but not least, the high speeds of travel would make it hard for an emergency response team to do its job properly—something that has not really been discussed as much as it should. In the present, there is no proposal on the table for the Big Apple. Nevertheless, the Boring Company has plenty of work to keep it busy for at least a couple of years with or without a New York City construction project.

---

[143] Neil Strauss (2017), "Elon Musk: The Architect of Tomorrow," *Rolling Stone.*

Not-A- Flamethrower

Believe it or not, this dubious product that is clearly a flamethrower, despite its name, was the product that marked the company's debut. It sold at its pickup party, with many of those sales being pre-orders and reservations. Obviously, the perfect addition for a mariachi band, churros, and Capri Sun drinks was such a baffling product, at least for a firm that came out of Musk's weirdly wired mind.

The idea of the Not-A-Flamethrower came to Musk in December 2017, when he tweeted: "After 50k hats, we'll start selling The Boring Company Flamethrower." The famous hats were the company's first massive merch product that sold like hotcakes, which ultimately led to the flamethrower becoming a real product. Surprisingly, the "unique" merch that followed in the footsteps of the hats was proven to be even more popular. It was up for sale on January 27, 2018, and by February 1 it sold out.

Why hats and flamethrowers? Because obviously, they sell, or rather because they are very in tune with Elon's quirkiness. The inspiration for the fiery product might have struck him at a Beyoncé concert where he tweeted: "I love indoor flamethrowers." The flamethrower seems to have two purposes: it allows fans to show their loyalty, and its proof that Musk can get whatever he wants, no matter how outlandish it may sound.

What are people going to do with the flamethrowers? Most likely keep them as a "cool" display item even if there are some brave Musk fans out there that will probably find an actual use for the thing, like some very extreme cooking or who-knows-what. After all, the "boring" flamethrower is not that powerful to be actually labeled as a flamethrower, which would require a permit to own and use. It's rather comparable with a propane torch, so it's mostly safe if used wisely. It is also easy to use. You just need to get the gas going, press the ignition switch, and then pull the trigger.

The majority of people don't really care about the use of it or its purpose. It's an interesting product with an appealing design, and most importantly, it's fun. As Amira Yahyaoui, a big fan that was at the pickup party, told a journalist: "I love what Elon Musk does and how he thinks.

The moment it went out, I was like, buy, buy, buy."[144] As of its purpose, Amira confessed, "I didn't buy it to burn things. I bought it to have the object. I think it's something to collect."[145]

It's all about Musk—the people just can't get enough of him. Whatever crazy product he'll come up with in the future, there will most likely be a market for it. Because it's an Elon Musk exclusive, and that's all the public wants.

---

[144] Elizabeth Lopatto (2018), "I Have a Boring Company Not-A-Flamethrower," *The Verge*.
[145] Elizabeth Lopatto (2018), "I Have a Boring Company Not-A-Flamethrower," *The Verge*.

Chapter 11: Pravduh.com

Pravduh started off just like the majority of Musk's ideas: on a whim. On May 23, 2018, he tweeted: "Going to create a site where the public can rate the core truth of any article & track the credibility score over time of each journalist, editor & publication. Thinking of calling it Pravda." Pravda is actually a Russian word that means "truth," and it's also the name of the Soviet Communist newspaper. Musk intends to use the site to reveal the truth to the people as he believes that media companies "lay claim to the truth, but publish only enough to sugarcoat the lie, which is why the public no longer respects them."

Musk truly believes that the media focuses only on the negative "stories" about Tesla and many other subjects. Regarding his motivation, he explained that the journalists are not at fault as they "are under constant pressure to get max clicks & earn advertising dollars or get fired." But for Tesla, especially, this creates a "tricky situation, as Tesla doesn't advertise, but fossil fuel companies & gas/diesel car companies are among world's biggest advertisers."

His point is that if Tesla does not advertise, the people are left to believe whatever the media feeds them, and the media is focused on negatives as they were more efficient in gaining the people's attention and interest. In a small Twitter feed, he explained why "pravda" became "pravduh" in the end:

1. "Tried to buy http://Pravda.com, but Russia said no. Turns out they already use it."

2. "Turns out http://Pravda.com is actually owned by Ukraine. For some reason, Russia didn't bother to correct me."

3. "Problem solved was able to buy http://Pravduh.com! Game on."

The site is mainly a platform where journalists and reporters can be "rated" based on how thoughtful their articles are. It also questions the credibility of publications. Pravduh.com, just as many others of Musk's idea, gathers admirers as well as critics. Some think that the site could be used to willingly affect negatively someone's career and even abuse them. On the other side, his claims raised a new question: What if he was right? What if media outlets really use their influence to put Tesla in a bad light despite its achievements and merits?

CleanTechnica, a world-renowned cleantech-focused website, decided to take the matter into its own hands and do some research to discover the truth of "pravduh." Vijai Govindan and Chanan Bos split their research in two (the major websites) to make sure it's as accurate as possible, and they started digging.

Govindan noticed that Bloomberg was on top when it came to Tesla-related headlines, out of which the majority were negative. By going deeper, he noticed that the site had a liking toward reusing the same headline, each time choosing to portray it negatively.

He gave those three headlines as an example:

1. "Saudi Fund Breathes New Life into Lucid after Going Mum on Musk"
2. "Tesla (TSLA) Rival Lucid's Saudi Funding Is Ominous"
3. "Tesla Rival Lucid to Receive $1 Billion from Saudi Wealth Fund"

All those articles speak about the same incident, Lucid receiving a founding from Saudi Wealth Fund, and somehow, Bloomberg managed to make it all about how Tesla will be affected by that and how this news is "ominous" for the electric car manufacturer. Another headline from Bloomberg, "Tesla Is Facing US Criminal Probe over Elon Musk Statements," is not shy at all to portray Tesla as a "criminal company" even if, at that time, it was based on speculations and dubious "unnamed sources." Govindan highlights that in this situation, even if Tesla is found innocent, the reputation of the company is already tarnished, which could or could not negatively affect sales.

For Bloomberg, though, all this negativity could have a logical explanation. A *Business Insider* article by Julia La Roche talked about Bloomberg's policy of rewarding reporters that "move the market," a practice that is more than unusual in the business. In other words, stories that are perceived as "sensational" will make the reporter more plausible for a hefty annual bonus—whether or not the articles speaks "the truth" or just throws in rumors or "scoops" or if the headline is misleading. Regarding their incentive policies, Bloomberg declared, "It isn't news unless it's true. At Bloomberg News, the most important news is actionable. That means we strive to be first to report surprises in markets that change behavior, and we put a premium on reporting that reveals the biggest changes in relative value across all assets."[146]

Whether or not there's foul play against Tesla at Bloomberg, Govindan could not say, but it does seem that some news outlets don't dabble as much as they should in the accuracy of their information.

While Govindan frowned upon the misdeeds of Bloomberg, Chanan Bos looked at all massive publications in order to assess how many Tesla-related articles they had and whether or not they were predominantly negative. Take CNBC, for example. Out of 293 articles on Tesla, around 129 were negative, 75 neutral, and 89 positive, which means that CNBC is quite balanced. However, some news outlets really stand out as having an overwhelmingly negative approach to Tesla-related news.

Here are some examples:

- CNN—out of 70 articles on Tesla, 43 were negative, 14 neutral, and 13 positive

- *The New York Times*—out of 31 articles on Tesla, 21 were negative, 7 neutral, and 3 positive

- Gizmo—out of 16 articles on Tesla, 11 were negative, 4 neutral, and 1 positive

No matter how you look at it, the focus is on the negative, even for those news outlets that don't have that many articles on Tesla at all, such as Gizmo. Why? Maybe because those stories sell more, and Tesla has a fair share of mistakes that can be fructified in the long term.

---

[146] Julia La Roche (2013), "Bloomberg News Pays Reporters More If Their Stories Move Markets," *Business Insider.*

Chanan Bos is a real Musk admirer and has a deep respect for Elon and Tesla, but he did not let that influence his research. He just presented some numbers and is up to the readers to pull their own conclusions. Is it all a conspiracy to make Tesla look bad? That's unlikely and usually not the case. It's just that, stories that "move the market," as Bloomberg put it, sell. And there are plenty of people out there that would like to see Tesla fail.

So Musk had his right to be frustrated by the media coverage of his electric car company. Pravduh might come in as a tool to clear up some misunderstanding and clearly show where there is bias against Tesla, or it may be used as a means of destroying people's careers, which is something that Musk does not condone. Either way, it's an interesting idea coming from the guy that dreams about life on Mars, and it has the potential of changing the way people perceive media outlets.

Chapter 12: Investments

Elon Musk is a man of many interests. Sure, he might be upfront and personal with some fields, like aerospace, energy, and transportation; but he's also a supporter of e-commerce companies, the biotech industry, and AI development. For some companies that adhere to one of those fields, he was (and for some still is) a major investor as a part of his struggle to "change the world for the better."

Everdream

Everdream is a digital-content agency founded by Lyndon Rive and Russ Rive, who are Musk's cousins. It provides software services for personal computers and desktop managing. Basically, the firm enabled its customers to manage their PCs from anywhere around the world without implementing high prices. Musk invested $1 million in it in 2002. In 2007, the company was bought by Dell, and it became one of its subsidiaries.

David Frink, a spokesperson for Dell, said about the company: "We think it's a great step for Dell's expansion of its service capabilities to help customers and channel partners simplify their IT department. This is a company that's got advanced capabilities in remote service management for small, medium and large businesses. It's got both remote tracking of hardware and software assets, and allows for distribution of software updates and patches across your company's infrastructure from a remote location."[147]

After the sale, Lyndon would go on to found Solar City.

Game Trust

Game Trust is an online gaming app developer that produced software for multiplayer games. It has a Game Frame platform that could manage tournaments, game configuration, monitoring, as well as registra-

---

[147] Andy Patrizio (2007), "Dell Acquires Remote Management Form Everdream," *Internet News.*

tions and security issues. Besides mobile apps, it works with PC and console systems. It was founded by Adeo Ressi, a former roommate of Musk. In 2005, Elon invested $1 million into the company, but the following year, he was voted off the board of directors. Game Trust was sold to Real Networks in the year 2007.

Mahalo

Mahalo was a web directory and internet-based knowledge exchange that built handcrafted result sets for many popular search terms as a way of distinguishing itself from Google. Mahalo also offered how-to guides. Musk was a lead investor, putting $2 million into the company. In 2014, Jason Calacanis, the founder, announced that while the focus of the company will shift toward the app Inside, which summarized and highlighted top news stories, Mahalo still made seven figures, so they were not shutting it off, but there was no intention to further invest in it.

However, the website was shut down, and Mahalo disappeared as soon as it made its apparition on the market.

One Riot

One Riot is a network of mobile apps that analyze social media activity in order to target apps. It was founded in 2006, and one of its founders was Kimbal, Musk's brother, who acted as a CEO. It had many big-name employers, such as AT&T, the Gap, and Toyota. Clients could execute media campaigns directly to One Riot's network or use the data to advertise across other sources of mobile inventory. The potential customers were targeted by their interests and demographics. One Riot could also define geo-locations, offering a full-package kind of deal.

Musk invested $2.5 million into the company. In 2011, it was purchased by Walmart Labs.

Halcyon Molecular

Founded by brothers William and Michael Andregg in 2008, the company was a whole genome sequencing start-up. Halcyon Molecular benefited by having a lot of big investors from the get-go, such as Elon Musk, who invested the big sum of $10 million, and the Founders

Fund. Halcyon had big dreams, such as being able to "sequence 100 percent complete human genome in less than ten minutes for less than $100" which for anyone's perspective was overly ambitious. In 2013, their sequencing paradigm was praised as it "showed great potential as a high-throughput DNA manipulation technology" according to Harvard's George M. Church, but it also needed a lot of work if they ever wanted to safely use it in scaled DNA sequencing.

In 2012, it shut down after competition got ahead of it, bringing newer, cheaper, and safer technologies to the market.

DeepMind

DeepMind is a British AI company founded in 2010 by many venture capitalists such as Elon Musk, who invested $1.65 million in it.

They started by teaching AI how to play old games (from the '70s and '80s, such as Space Invaders and Breakout), which are much simpler than today's gaming options. The games were introduced one by one without the program having any prior knowledge regarding them. "The cognitive processes which the AI goes through are said to be very like those a human who had never seen the game would use to understand and attempt to master it," the company believed, and indeed, the AI would eventually ace the games after a period of learning.[148]

In 2014, the company was acquired by Google, and it also received the Company of the Year award from Cambridge Computers Laboratory. The future goal of DeepMind is to build powerful generalized learning algorithms and to create an AI that could be useful for anything. It will also focus more on the human brain as "attempting to distill intelligence into an algorithmic construct may prove to be the best path to understanding some of the enduring mysteries of our minds," according to Demis Hassabis, one of the founders.[149]

Stripe

Stripe is a technology company founded by Irish entrepreneurs John and Patrick Collison in 2010. It received numerous founding from Y

---

[148] Bernard Marr (2018), "How Google's Amazing AI Start–Up 'DeepMind' Is Making Our World A Smarter Place," *Forbes*.

[149] Demis Hassabis (2012), "Model the brain's algorithms," *Nature*.

Combinator, Sequoia Capital, and Elon Musk, who invested $10.2 million in 2011, among others. It is an online payment company that lets developers integrate payment processing into their websites without the need of having a merchant account. It also includes a billing product for online businesses.

In 2011, it launched a private beta, and in 2013, it acquired Kick-off, the chat and task-management application. In 2016, it launched its Atlas platform, which allows start-up companies to easily integrate in the United States. This platform was updated a couple of times since, and now it covers more countries such as Cuba, and it accepts the use of Delaware-based limited liability companies.

Stripe has big plans for the future, such as creating a platform for companies to issue Visa and Mastercard credit cards and many others.

Vicarious

Vicarious is an artificial intelligence company founded in 2010 by D. Scott Phoenix and Dr. Dileep George. The two wish to build software that can "think and learn like a human" by using theorized computational principles of the brain. It received plenty of funding from companies and renowned individuals. Some examples include Founders Fund, Zarco Investment Group, Elon Musk, Mark Zuckerberg, Ashton Kutcher, Jeff Bezos, and Marc Benioff. Musk alone invested $2 million in the project.

In 2013, Vicarious announced that their AI was able to solve modern CAPTCHAs, a challenge-response test that determines if the user is human or not, with a recognition rate of over 90 percent. Luis von Ahn, a founder of reCAPTCHA, declared his skepticism, saying, "It's hard for me to be impressed since I see these every few months," as it was not the first time some company made big claims.[150]

However, the success of Vicarious is based on their insight into the human brain, and the use of the Recursive Cortical Network, which is a visual perception system that is able to interpret images and videos in the same manner as a human would. The future is bright for Vicarious, and people can't wait to see what they will achieve next.

---

[150] Robert Hof: "AI Startup Vicarious Claims Milestone in Quest to Build a Brain: Cracking CAPTCHA," *Forbes.*

Hyperloop Transportation Technologies

After Musk came with the Hyperloop idea in 2013 and made it free for anyone to try out, many companies accepted the challenge. HTT was founded in November of the same year, with the clear goal of turning Elon's concept into a feasible transportation method. It was founded via crowd collaboration, and Musk himself invested $15,000 into the new company, hoping to see his Hyperloop brought to life. HTT is a bold company that affirmed on more than one occasion to be only ten years away from a commercial version of the Hyperloop.

Since the founding, the company kept growing at a slow pace. With each year came new experienced employees and beneficial partnerships offers. As of 2018, HTT already has plenty of projects on its hands from agreements to take future routes into consideration to full-on construction contracts.

NeuroVigil

NeuroVigil is a neurodiagnostic company that provides the technology capable of reading brain wave data. It was founded in 2007 by Dr. Phillip Low, and since then, it has created the iBrain, a portable platform for neural monitoring and analysis. It is widely used to monitor neuropathologies, such as epilepsy, Alzheimer's, Parkinson's, and many others. The iBrain is also used to observe how the brain responds to drugs that affect it and as a treatment when it comes to restoring lost functions. NeuroVigil has a lot of potential for the future as their iBrain product alone made a big difference in the medical world. Even NASA uses it to track astronauts on the International Space Station.

Elon Musk invested $500,000 is the company in 2015.

Surrey Satellite Technology

Musk supports the "world's leading small-satellite manufacturer," Surrey Satellite Technology, as they proved the world that small inexpensive satellites that can be built much faster (thanks to their size) can be successfully used in complex missions. The company prides itself with its "use of new technologies" and with its status as a pioneer in the small satellite market. With thirty years of experience to back it up, small as its satellites may be, Surrey is one company to not be taken lightly.

Future of Life Institute

The Future of Life Institute is a research and outreach organization run by volunteers. It was founded in 2014 by cosmologist Mark Tegmark, along with a group of highly gifted individuals. Their board of advisors consists of big names, such as the late Stephen Hawking (prior to his death), Morgan Freeman, Frank Wilczek, Stuart J. Russell, and Elon Musk.

The main purpose of the company is to mitigate the existential risks facing humanity, especially from advanced AI.

In 2015, it organized a conference that discussed the future of AI, both the opportunities and the risks that it may bring. The goal was to find research directions that would lead to maximizing future benefits of artificial intelligence and to assess safety concerns. In the same year, the foundation announced that Elon Musk has made a donation of $10 million to found a potential global AI research venture. As of 2018, the Future of Life Institute prevails in its endeavors of researching artificial intelligence and assessing all the possible negative outcomes that might come from AI development.

XPRIZE Foundation

XPRIZE is a nonprofit organization that creates and manages competitions that encourage the development of technologies that would benefit humanity. The competitions are high-profile to motivate both individuals and companies to join the game of coming up with innovative ideas to solve the problems that mankind faces.

The foundation has multiple goals, such as finding investors willing to support futuristic ideas, promoting the idea of innovation, and unifying people from all around the world regardless of their nationality or education in the quest of helping the evolution of humanity.

Below are some of the events and prizes led by the foundation:

- XPRIZE for Suborbital Spaceflight—it incentivized the building of private spaceships and promoted space programs.

- Wendy Schmidt Oil Cleanup XCHALLENGE—it sought to inspire a new generation to come up with solutions that would clean up oil spills faster.

- Progressive Insurance Automotive XPRIZE—it supported the design, manufacturing, and racing of cars that release a minimum of emissions, which led to the creation of many electric vehicles.

- Water Abundance XPRIZE—it promoted both the development of a machine that extracted water only by using renewable energy, making the extraction cheaper. It also raised awareness of the scarcity of water in developing countries

Elon Musk is a benefactor of the Global Learning XPRIZE, to which he donated $15 million in 2017 with a purpose of developing teaching methods for the children who don't have access to education. It challenges participants to come up with open-source software that would enable young kids to learn basics, such as reading, writing, and arithmetic without adult supervision or assistance.

The movement had a big impact on the illiteracy rate, and in 2019, Matt Keller, a senior director of the Global learning XPRIZE, declared, "I see this as the end of the beginning. Within the next decade, my hope is that children will have access to a device or platform that they can speak to, that knows what the child likes, and knows what the child does and does not know. It will be so entwined with that child's life that it could become their mentor as they matriculate through school, just as a parent or teacher would. That is the future we hope happens because it is the only solution that scales to reach every child."[151]

Musk Foundation

Elon Musk wasted no time to start a "foundation" of his own in order to support the areas that he finds of interest, and in the early days of his career (the year 2001 to be more exact), the Musk Foundation was born.

---

[151] Peter High (2018), "Elon Musk-funded XPRIZE Is One Step Closer to Ending Global Illiteracy," *Forbes*.

The website of the foundation consists of only a few rows of to-the-point writing:

Musk Foundation. Grants are made in support of the following:

- Renewable energy research and advocacy
- Human space exploration research and advocacy
- Pediatric research
- Science and engineering education
- Development of safe artificial intelligence to benefit humanity

No fancy fonts, no self-praising ode, no photos showcasing a smiling benevolent figure. Just a simple declaration. According to documents obtained by *The Guardian*, the Musk Foundation reached far beyond those fields, all of them very in tune with Musk's preferences, the biggest founding going into one of his favorite subjects: artificial intelligence.

The foundation is private, and he is the sole provider for it, using it for most of his charitable ventures. It helped about 160 different charities, and it distributed more than $54 million to those in need—many going toward educational, environmental, medical, and space organizations. The foundation also helped institutions close to Musk's heart, such as a charity managed by his brother, the Mirman School for Gifted Children (attended by his children) and an art project at the Burning Man Festival.

He launched the foundation alongside his brother Kimbal, who acted as its secretary. The first "investment" that he made to the foundation was 30,000 eBay shares, valued at $2.1 million. In this first era of the organization, the foundation made donations to educational charities, children's hospitals, and Musk's former schools, colleges, universities from South Africa and the United States.

As the foundation's capital grew, so did its donations. With some help from his solar-power company, Solar City, Musk's foundation funded photovoltaic systems to help the communities affected by the Fukushima earthquake and the Deepwater Horizon Disaster. In 2010, the foundation supported the launch of the Kitchen Community charity.

Kitchen Community, which would later become known as Big Green, was Kimbal's idea, and it consisted of creating "learning gardens," which would help children grow and prepare their own fresh food. Up to this day, this is one of the foundation's biggest investment.

In 2012, Musk signed the Giving Pledge, which is a commitment to give away the bulk of your wealth during your lifetime or upon death. Many of the world's richest individuals swore off their riches, such as Warren Buffet and Michael Bloomberg. For Elon Musk, the decision was a no-brainer. It led to an expansion of his foundation, which means that the Musk Foundation started to support causes like the Los Angeles Police Foundation, the Rock and Roll Hall of Fame, and a not-for-profit women's organization supporting professional New York women from public-oriented industries, such as digital media, film, and television. The foundation also made a big $10,000 donation to a nonprofit organization that researched the medical use of marijuana and MDMA called the Multidisciplinary Association for Psychedelic Studies. The donation funded the creation of The Temple of Whollyness, the piece of art made from wood that went up in flame at that year's Burning Man festival.

In 2015, the capital of the foundation was running on fumes, so Musk donated Tesla shares worth $225 million to make sure it keeps on going. His first instinct from that point was to donate to organizations that researched the development of safe artificial intelligence programs. "Elon's charitable giving has kick-started AI safety research, transforming it into what is now a vibrant and respectable research area," commented Max Tegmark, one of the founders of the Future of Life Institute, regarding Musk's role in the AI industry.[152] A clear example is his involvement with OpenAI.

In 2016, the Musk Foundation made one of its biggest donation—$37.8 million to Vanguard Charitable, a donor-advised fund and tax-efficient vehicle that holds money on behalf of its clients and anonymously distributes it over time to various charities or causes. Musk strongly believes that the best kind of philanthropy is that which lays hidden from the public's eyes and dwells in anonymity. The use of Vanguard makes

---

[152] Mark Harris (2019), "How Elon Musk's secretive foundation Hands out his billions," *The Guardian.*

it very hard to know exactly what the Musk Foundation, an organization that's already shy about sharing its deeds with the public, is up to. According to Musk, lately, the foundation is focused on solving the public health crisis in Flint, with donations consisting of water filtration equipment and laptops having already been made.

Elon Musk has never accepted any form of compensation for his work with the foundation.

Chapter 13: Dating Life

Being a billionaire does not guarantee that you will get a perfect life. Money can't buy everything, and love is one of those abstract concepts that just happens at certain times, without much logic to back it up and almost impossible to explain. It's even harder to enjoy your romantic story when you have so many businesses to attend to and projects to bring to life. Elon Musk had his fair share of failed relationships, but he has not given up on love, not just yet. He told the *Rolling Stone*, "If I'm not in love, if I'm not with a long-term companion, I cannot be happy. I will never be happy without having someone. Going to sleep alone kills me. It's not like I don't know what that feels like: Being in a big empty house, and the footsteps echoing through the hallway, no one there— and no one on the pillow next to you. F——. How do you make yourself happy in a situation like that?"

Despite his money and fame, it's love that makes him happy, according to him. However, some of his late partners tell another story—one of a man married to his job to the point of obsession. It's hard to tell the truth from speculation when you're seeing a relationship from the outside. You can never know the real dynamics of a relationship if you're not an active part of it, and even so, your opinion might be very subjective.

Celebrity relationships are often a case of "he said, she said." The truth is somewhere in the middle.

Justine Wilson

Musk met his soon-to-be first wife while they both were at Queen's University. She recalls that he was the one to make the first move by inviting her out for some ice cream. Although she decided against it, he just went ahead and showed up at her place with "two chocolate-chip ice cream cones dripping down his hands."

To Musk, in those early years of his life, Justine was everything he wanted: "an intellectual with an edge," strong, "semi-bohemian," and one of the most beautiful women in the campus. She was a dreamer that wished for a passionate romance, but as fate has it, "what she fell for instead was a relentless, ambitious geek." They shared a class together, abnormal psychology, where he showed his type-A personality. Despite his love for competing with Justine, he was also romantic at times. He once sent her a dozen roses, each with its own written note, and he also gifted her a copy of *The Prophet*, a book of poetry, which had handwritten romantic notes all over it.

When he transferred to Wharton, their relationship got cold, even if he occasionally sent her flowers. According to Maye, Justine was "hip" and dated other guys while they were apart, which was hard on Elon. He also tried to see other girls, but Justine was always the one in his heart. And he came back to her, full force. "He would call very insistently," she said. "You always knew it was Elon because the phone would never stop ringing. The man does not take no for an answer. You can't blow him off. I do think of him as the Terminator. He locks his gaze on to something and says, 'It shall be mine.' Bit by bit, he won me over," Justine told Ashlee Vance.[153]

They met again after she graduated, and they rekindled their relationship. At that time, she was working on her first novel while he was trying to put Zip2 on its feet.

Justine told *Marie Claire US*, "After graduation, he'd moved to Silicon Valley. He was sharing an apartment in Mountain View with three roommates and building his first dot-com company, Zip2. I soon flew out for the first of many visits. One night, over dinner, he asked me how many kids I wanted to have. 'One or two,' I said immediately. 'Although if I could afford nannies, I'd like to have 4.' He laughed. 'That's the difference between you and me,' he said. 'I just assume that there will be nannies.' He made a rocking motion with his arms and said, happily, 'Baby.'"

Allegedly, he stole her heart by allowing her to buy as many books as she liked with his credit card since she was an avid reader. After the

---

[153] Ashlee Vance (2015), "Elon Musk: Tesla, SpaceX, and the Quest for a Fantastic Future," page 31.

sale of Zip2, Musk was able to buy a place of his own so he could focus more on his relationship with Justine. "We fought a lot, but when
we weren't fighting, there was a deep sense of compassion—a bond,"
she told Ashlee Vance.[154] One of the main reason for their fight was his
jealousy. Justine kept getting calls from an ex-boyfriend, and he hated
that. In frustration, she told him that if she has to put up with his jealousy fits, they might as well marry and get done with it. To which he responded by proposing on the spot—a proposal that would be re-en-
acted a few days later when Musk also gave her a ring. The pair got
married in the year 2000.

Because of the situation at X.com, the pair had to postpone their honeymoon to late December, when Musk arranged a trip. One week in
Brazil and one in a South African game reserve. But out of the blue,
disaster struck: Musk contracted falciparum malaria, the most dangerous type of malaria and the one that caused most malaria-related
deaths.

He was bedridden for a few days after they got back, and Justine, worried, sent him to the Sequoia Hospital. There, he had a near-death experience as doctors initially missed his diagnosis and treated him for a
wrong condition until someone that was more familiar with malaria rang
the alarm. Musk fought for his life and spent ten days in the intensive
care unit. His recovery took six months. While Musk treats it jokingly,
affirming that for him it was a lesson to not take any more vacations as
"they kill you," Justine was emotionally affected by the ordeal. "He's
built like a tank. He has a level of stamina and an ability to deal with
levels of stress that I've never seen in anyone else. To see him laid low
like that in total misery was like a visit to an alternate universe."[155]

What followed was a relocation to Los Angeles as Musk reached his
thirtieth birthday and realized he wanted a change. He was no longer a
"child prodigy," and the life in Silicon Valley started to lose its charms.
He was sick of start-ups, fed up with never-ending talks about founding
and becoming rich. Justine was looking forward to going out of that Silicon Valley lifestyle. "I had friends who complained that their husbands

---

[154] Ashlee Vance (2015), "Elon Musk: Tesla, SpaceX, and the Quest for a Fantastic Future,"
page 54.
[155] Ashlee Vance (2015), "Elon Musk: Tesla, SpaceX, and the Quest for a Fantastic Future,"
page 55.

came home at seven or eight. Elon would come home at eleven and work some more. People didn't always get the sacrifice he made in order to be where he was."[156] Los Angeles had the allure of a new place, a bigger "stage" for Musk to take his ambitions onto. "There's an element to him that likes the style and the excitement and color of a place like LA. Elon likes to be where the action is," Justine further explained the decision.[157]

Soon came the birth of their first son, Nevada Alexander Musk. Unfortunately, the child died at the age of ten weeks of sudden infant death syndrome.

Justine reminisced the painful moment: "The sale of PayPal vaulted Elon's net worth to well over $100 million. The same week, Nevada went down for a nap, placed on his back as always, and stopped breathing. He was ten weeks old, the age when male infants are most susceptible to SIDS. By the time the paramedics resuscitated him, he had been deprived of oxygen for so long that he was brain-dead. He spent three days on life support in a hospital in Orange County before we made the decision to take him off it. I held him in my arms when he died."

Musk was allegedly so shaken by the infant's death that he chose to deal with it on his own. Justine declared, "Elon made it clear that he did not want to talk about Nevada's death. I didn't understand this, just as he didn't understand why I grieved openly, which he regarded as 'emotionally manipulative.'"[158]

He opened up to Ashlee Vance about his take on the terrible situation: "It made me extremely sad to talk about it. I'm not sure why I'd want to talk about extremely sad events. It does no good for the future. If you've got other kids and obligations, then wallowing in sadness does no good for anyone around you. I'm not sure what should be done in such situations."[159]

---

[156] Ashlee Vance (2015), "Elon Musk: Tesla, SpaceX, and the Quest for a Fantastic Future," page 57.

[157] Ashlee Vance (2015), "Elon Musk: Tesla, SpaceX, and the Quest for a Fantastic Future," page 57.

[158] Ashlee Vance (2015), "Elon Musk: Tesla, SpaceX, and the Quest for a Fantastic Future," page 66.

After that, with the aid of in vitro fertilization, they had five sons—twins Griffin and Xavier in 2004 and triplets Kai, Saxon, and Damian in 2006. In her essay to *Marie Claire*, she spoke about the decision of becoming a mother again: "I buried my feelings, coping with Nevada's death by making my first visit to an IVF clinic less than 2 months later. Elon and I planned to get pregnant again as swiftly as possible. Within the next 5 years, I gave birth to twins, then triplets, and I sold 3 novels to Penguin and Simon & Schuster."

Musk felt very attached to his children, often calling them "the love of my life," and spending as much time as possible with them.

As Musk became more and more of a public figure, their life changed. They brought a house in Bel Air, and they had famous neighbors. They started to be invited to important social events. "We had a domestic staff of five. During the day, our home transformed into a workplace. We went to black-tie fundraisers and got the best tables at elite Holly- wood nightclubs, with Paris Hilton and Leonardo DiCaprio partying next to us. When Google co-founder Larry Page got married on Richard Branson's private Caribbean island, we were there, hanging out in a villa with John Cusack and watching Bono pose with swarms of adoring women outside the reception tent."[160] Justine offered a look into their life at the time through a magazine article.

Justine loved the popular life more than Elon did. As a fiction writer, she loved to post stories about the life of her family in a blog she kept. Of course, the stories were filled with the author's own liberties regard- ing facts, but it still served as overall documentation of their daily activi- ties. Musk was the type to keep his personal life to himself, and Justine seemed to be the opposite. She liked making an adventure out of their public outings. About a party that Elon attended, for Joe Francis's birth- day, Justine wrote: "E was there for a bit but admitted he also found it 'kind of lame'—he's been to a couple of parties at NN's house now and ends up feeling self-conscious, 'because it just seems like there are al- ways these skeevy guys wandering around the house trolling for girls. I

---

[159] Ashlee Vance (2015), "Elon Musk: Tesla, SpaceX, and the Quest for a Fantastic Future," page 66.

[160] Ashlee Vance (2015), "Elon Musk: Tesla, SpaceX, and the Quest for a Fantastic Future," page 117.

don't want to be seen as one of those guys.'"[161] NN was the acronym that she used for Francis, meaning "notorious neighbor," as he was indeed their neighbor and a famous person.

The blog provided a nice glimpse into the eccentric CEO's life, and to the public, he came off as "charming." The media liked his image and described him as being "part playboy, part space cowboy." Thanks to Justine's hobby, the world learned that Musk's nickname was Elonius and that he loved to place wagers (usually one-dollar ones) on small weird things when he was sure he'd win. "This was E's I'm-thinking-about-a-rocket-problem stance, which makes me pretty sure that he had just gotten some kind of bothersome work-related e-mail and was clearly oblivious to the fact that a picture was being taken at all. This is also the reason I get suck [sic] a kick out of it—the spouse the camera caught is the exact spouse I encountered, say, last 10 night en route to the bathroom, standing in the hallway frowning with his arms folded," she wrote once to describe Musk's expression in a picture that the press used.[162] Needless to say, Musk was not very happy with how open Justine was in her blog posts.

As Tesla and SpaceX started having troubles, the media latched on Musk. To make matters worse, his marriage with Justine started to crumble, and she started bringing their personal problems to her blog for the whole world to see. She felt that the people in his entourage treated her as Musk's "ornament" and the mother of his kids rather than a woman with a career of her own. She demanded that he acknowledge her as a writer and present her accordingly to new people, something that he handled rather poorly. He simply told people, "Justine wants me to tell you that she's written novels," which only infuriated her more.[163]

According to Justine, Musk is a complete workaholic. Even when not physically there, his mind kept wandering off to the office and its responsibilities. The matters at Tesla and SpaceX consumed him so

---

[161] Ashlee Vance (2015), "Elon Musk: Tesla, SpaceX, and the Quest for a Fantastic Future," page 117.

[162] Ashlee Vance (2015), "Elon Musk: Tesla, SpaceX, and the Quest for a Fantastic Future," pages 117–118.

[163] Ashlee Vance (2015), "Elon Musk: Tesla, SpaceX, and the Quest for a Fantastic Future," page 119.

much that he was constantly working, all while Justine longed for their early days' romance. Allegedly, she had no idea that in that period they were struggling financially. He kept her in the dark most likely to shelter her from the harsh reality.

But Antonio Gracias, the CEO of Valor Equity and one of Musk's best friends, knew the situation. Regarding that time of financial strain and marital tension, Gracias recalled Musk's thoughts that he expressed over dinner: "Things were starting to be difficult with Justine, but they were still together. During that dinner, Elon said, 'I will spend my last dollar on these companies. If we have to move into Justine's parents' basement, we'll do it.'"[164]

He treated his marriage as a business merger. On the day of their wedding, he made it clear that he was "the alpha," and he also made her sign a prenuptial contract that was rather unfair to her. Basically, she signed away her rights as a spouse, and she would have no legal claim over money or property in the situation of a divorce. Justine confessed that at that point she "shrugged it off," but with time, she understood that his visions will become problematic for their relationship.

"He had grown up in the male-dominated culture of South Africa, and the will to compete and dominate that made him so successful in business did not magically turn off when he came home," she later described him.[165] They often had arguments where they would snap at each other with her reminding him that she was not his employee and him letting her know that, if that was the case, he would have fired her long ago.

Despite her hopes that the relationship will last, it was not meant to be.

In 2008, Musk filed for divorce, announcing her only weeks after that he fell in love with someone else, Talulah Riley, a British actress with whom he was already engaged.

Right before the divorce happened, she made a blog post that was the harbinger of the news to come: "Divorce, for me, was like the bomb you set off when all other options have been exhausted. I had not yet given

---

[164] Ashlee Vance (2015), "Elon Musk: Tesla, SpaceX, and the Quest for a Fantastic Future," page 119.
[165] Jessie Stephens (2018), "It's Elon's World and the Rest of Us Live in It—What It's Like to Be Married to Elon Musk," *MamaMia.*

up on the diplomacy option, which was why I hadn't already filed. We were still in the early stages of marital counseling (three sessions total). Elon, however, took matters into his own hands—he tends to like to do that—when he gave me an ultimatum: 'Either we fix [the marriage] today, or I will divorce you tomorrow.' That night, and again the next morning, he asked me what I wanted to do. I stated emphatically that I was not ready to unleash the dogs of divorce; I suggested that "we" hold off for at least another week. Elon nodded, touched the top of my head, and left. Later that same morning I tried to make a purchase and discovered that he had cut off my credit card, which is when I also knew that he had gone ahead and filed (as it was, E did not tell me directly; he had another person do it)."[166]

This bomb of a post was followed up by a neutrally toned short entry after the divorce went public: "We had a good run. We married young, took it as far as we could and now it is over."[167] The nasty divorce put a strain on their relationships, with him going as far as handling his children via an assistant.

In a *Business Insider* essay, he talked about his kids: "Custody of our 5 children is split evenly. Almost all of my non-work waking hours are spent with my boys, and they are the love of my life. I almost never take vacations, apart from kid-related travel." In an interview for Ashlee Vance's book, he went on to add: "I'm a pretty good dad. I have the kids for slightly more than half the week and spend a fair bit of time with them. I also take them with me when I go out of town."

Justine did not accept the divorce without fighting for her rights. Despite signing off a postnuptial agreement, she believed that she was entitled to a "fair divorce settlement." The media sided with Justine as her requests were not out of the ordinary. In order to reach an agreement, she ultimately settled for the house that they were living in, $2 million, and a hefty monthly alimony and child support for seventeen years. In an iron jive, she also got a Tesla Roadster.

---

[166] Ashlee Vance (2015), "Elon Musk: Tesla, SpaceX, and the Quest for a Fantastic Future," page 120.
[167] Ashlee Vance (2015), "Elon Musk: Tesla, SpaceX, and the Quest for a Fantastic Future," page 119.

However, in a funny twist of fate, though Justine and Musk's relationship was unbearable, the first wife and the second wife ended up becoming friends, with Justine making the first step toward getting along by sending her an email: "I would rather live out the French-movie version of things, in which the two women become friends and various philosophies are pondered."

Later on, Justine Wilson will describe her marriage to Musk as "oppressive," with her having to cater to his needs and him not being as involved as he should in his family's life.

She kept on writing Musk-related articles on her blog, which sometimes mentioned Riley or the type of parenting that Musk adhered to. One of her posts, which revealed that Musk had forbidden his boys to play with stuffed toys after they turned seven, ended up putting him in a bad light, media criticizing him. As a testimony of the love she once felt for him, Justine stepped in to defend him: "Elon is hard-core. He grew up in a tough culture and tough circumstances. He had to become very tough to not only thrive but to conquer the world. He doesn't want to raise soft over-privileged kids with no direction."[168]

Talulah Riley

After Musk's divorce, Riley moved to Los Angeles to be closer to her fiancé, and in 2010, they went ahead and tied the knot.

Their first meeting was at a club, Whisky Mist in Mayfair, where Musk went with a friend. "I remember thinking that this guy probably didn't get to talk to young actresses a lot and that he seemed quite nervous. I decided to be really nice to him and give him a nice evening. Little did I know that he'd spoken to a lot of pretty girls in his life," Riley reminisced.[169]

Musk's side of the story behind their first meeting goes as follows: "She did look great, but what was going through my mind was 'Oh, I guess they are a couple of models.' You know, you can't actually talk to most models. You just can't have a conversation. But, you know, Talulah

---

[168] Ashlee Vance (2015), "Elon Musk: Tesla, SpaceX, and the Quest for a Fantastic Future," page 121.

[169] Ashlee Vance (2015), "Elon Musk: Tesla, SpaceX, and the Quest for a Fantastic Future," page 121.

was really interested in talking about rockets and electric cars. That was the interesting thing."[170]

Although she was a rising star at that time, Riley was just fresh out of her childhood home and into the glamorous world of celebrities. She was impressed enough by Musk to accept a date with him and go through with it despite finding out—from her father's internet search endeavor—that Musk was a married man. To his credit, he did mention his family and his status as a married man at the said date while not forgetting to add that a divorce was imminent. After the date, he invited her to see his rockets, video footage of them to be more precise, and he was taken enough with her to actually invite her to join him in the United States—an offer that she refused. They kept in touch, and soon after, Riley went for a visit to the City of Angels. For Riley, who was young, it all seemed like fun and games, but Musk took their impending relationship very seriously. In a matter of days, he dropped a proposal. "He said, 'I don't want you to leave. I want you to marry me.' I think I laughed. Then, he said, 'No. I'm serious. I'm sorry I don't have a ring.' I said, 'We can shake on it if you like.' And we did. I don't remember what I was thinking at the time, and all I can say is that I was twenty-two," Riley recalled.[171]

Riley's parents were not thrilled about their daughter marrying someone who not only was her senior by a lot but who also had a family—even if he was in the midst of a divorce. They did, however, love their daughter very much and wanted her to be happy, so they obliged. They even made the trip to America to meet their future son-in-law and give their blessing. Riley ended up having three engagement rings: a big flamboyant one, a subtle one that she could wear on an everyday basis, and a custom-made ring that was designed by Musk himself, which had a diamond surrounded by sapphires.

She later recalled that at the start of their relationship he "warned" her by saying that she was choosing "the hard path," referring to being with

[170] Ashlee Vance (2015), "Elon Musk: Tesla, SpaceX, and the Quest for a Fantastic Future," page 243.
[171] Ashlee Vance (2015), "Elon Musk: Tesla, SpaceX, and the Quest for a Fantastic Future," page 122.

him. She admitted that she "didn't quite understand at the time, but I do now. It's quite hard, quite the crazy ride."[172]

Riley was with him during the times of financial turmoil when he did not know if he could keep his both companies alive. But he was not willing to sacrifice any of them for the other to thrive, so he was under intense stress. He would sometimes share his worries with her, but most of the times, he let them eat him on the inside. According to Riley, he was in a very bad state. His sleeping schedule was a mess, his eating habits all over the place, and at all times, he seemed to be in physical pain. "He looked like death itself. I remember thinking this guy would have a heart attack and die. He seemed like a man on the brink," she described the financially burdened Musk.[173]

Gracias, Musk's good friend, painfully remembered how hard the year 2008 was for Musk. "He has the ability to work harder and endure more stress than anyone I've ever met. What he went through in 2008 would have broken anyone else. He didn't just survive. He kept working and stayed focused. Most people who are under that sort of pressure fray. Their decisions go bad. Elon gets hyper-rational. He's still able to make very clear long-term decisions. The harder it gets, the better he gets. Anyone who saw what he went through firsthand came away with more respect for the guy. I've just never seen anything like his ability to take pain."[174]

Regarding her stepmom experience for Musk's kids, Talulah told Ashlee Vance: "Elon is kind of cheeky and funny. He is very loving. He is devoted to his children. He is funny—really, really, really funny. He's quite mercurial. He's genuinely the oddest person I have ever met. He has moments of self-awareness and lucidity, which for me always bring him back around. He'll say something cheeky or funny and have this grin. He's smart in all sorts of areas. He's very well read and has this incredible wit. He loves movies. We went to see the new *Lego Movie*, and afterwards, he insisted on being referred to as Lord Business. He

---

[172] Ashlee Vance (2015), "Elon Musk: Tesla, SpaceX, and the Quest for a Fantastic Future," pages 122–123.

[173] Ashlee Vance (2015), "Elon Musk: Tesla, SpaceX, and the Quest for a Fantastic Future," page 127.

[174] Ashlee Vance (2015), "Elon Musk: Tesla, SpaceX, and the Quest for a Fantastic Future," page 129.

tries to come home early for family dinners with me and the kids and maybe play some computer games with the boys. They will tell us about their day, and we'll put them to bed. Then we'll chat and watch something together on the laptop, like *The Colbert Report.* On the weekends, we're traveling. The kids are good travelers. There were billions of nannies before. There was even a nanny manager. Things are a bit more normal now. We try and do stuff just as a family when we can. We have the kids four days a week. I like to say that I am the disciplinarian. I want them to have the sense of an ordinary life, but they live a very odd life. They were just on a trip with Justin Bieber. They go to the rocket factory and are like, 'Oh no, not again.' It's not cool if your dad does it. They're used to it."[175]

She went further to describe him and their relationship: "People don't realize that Elon has this incredible naiveté. There are certain times when he is incapable of anything other than pure joy. And then other times pure anger. When he feels something, he feels it so completely and purely. Nothing else can impose on it. There are so few people who can do that. If he sees something funny, he will laugh so loudly. He won't realize we are in a crowded theater and that other people are there. He is like a child. It's sweet and amazing. He says this random stuff like, 'I am a complicated man with very simple but specific needs' or 'No man is an island unless he is large and buoyant.' We make these lists of things we want to do. His latest contributions were to walk on a beach at sunset and whisper sweet nothings in each other's ear and to take more horseback rides. He likes reading, playing video games, and being with friends."[176]

In 2012, they filed for divorce, and he wrote her a heartfelt message on Twitter: "It was an amazing four years. I will love you forever. You will make someone very happy one day." But the split would not last, and soon, the two were seen together once again. By 2013, they were back to being married, once again, even if at that time rumors talked about Musk having a fling with Cameron Diaz—something that was never confirmed by any of them. Their relationship was a tumultuous one,

---

[175] Ashlee Vance (2015), "Elon Musk: Tesla, SpaceX, and the Quest for a Fantastic Future," page 280.

[176] Ashlee Vance (2015), "Elon Musk: Tesla, SpaceX, and the Quest for a Fantastic Future," page 280.

with another divorce being filed and withdrawn only a year after remarrying.

In 2016, Riley filed again for a divorce, and this time, they went through with it. Musk explained in a Forbes interview how they tried to save the marriage: "We took some time apart for several months to see if absence makes the heart grow fonder, and unfortunately, it did not. I still love her, but I'm not in love with her . . . I can't really give her what she wants."

Talulah and Musk remained on good terms, with her telling *People Magazine*: "We still see each other all the time and take care of each other."

Amber Heard

After the actress's divorce from Johnny Depp ended in 2016, she supposedly started a relationship with Musk. They were an odd pair, and they had the habit to break up and get back together due to busy schedules and differences. Their friendship was not hurt by them being romantically involved, and according to Musk and other sources, they still care about each other a lot, and the break-up was a mutual decision.

Regarding his failed relationship with Heard, Musk told *Rolling Stone*: "I was really in love, and it hurt bad."

As of 2019, Johnny Depp filed a lawsuit for defamation against Heard, as she claimed to have been abused by him, and he argues that she had a secret fling with Musk while they were still married. Depp also alleged that Musk visited Heard at night or when he was away, but Elon's representative denied all claims.

Claire Elise Boucher, a.k.a. Grimes

Musk kept his relationship with the Canadian singer secret until they attended the 2018 Met Gala together. Allegedly, they have met on Twitter in April of the same year after they discovered that they have made the same joke regarding AI on the blog LessWrong, which was about the Rococo Basilisk character in her "Flesh without Blood." Musk is also a fan of her music, occasionally tweeting some of her videos. In one occasion, he commented that her video was the "Best music video art I've seen in a while."

There were many jokes on the extent of their relationship, with someone going as far as to create a Chrome extension that replaced Elon Musk's name on a webpage with the phrase "Grime's boyfriend." Grimes supported and defended him on Twitter on more than one occasion.

They seemed to have broken up due to Tesla's shareholders mentioning her in their lawsuit against Musk and because of a Twitter feud with rapper Azealia Banks. The rapper was supposedly called to Los Angeles in order to collaborate with Grimes on a song, but she instead "waited around all weekend while Grimes coddled her boyfriend." Azealia went on to directly insult Musk and claim that he announce the privatization of Tesla only to "amuse his girlfriend," which instead denied ever meeting her. Speculations of a break-up appeared as they unfollowed each other on Twitter.

However, they were seen together in October at a pumpkin patch near Los Angeles, along with his kids. Then, at the time when Musk was launching his new Tesla Gigafactory in Shanghai, Grimes tweeted that she was "randomly in China" and asked about the "coolest things to do in Beijing and Shanghai," flaming up the rumors of them getting back together.

Neither Musk nor Grimes made any official statement regarding the actual status of their relationship.

Chapter 14: Politics

When it comes to politics, Elon Musk is an odd participant. Rather than adhering to one party, he's made donations to both Democrats and Republicans, which are pretty close to being equal. He's not one to go traditional and be a "loyal" advocate for one political view.

For example, he personally contributed to Hillary Clinton's campaign, but he was also part of Trump's economic advisory board in 2017. He is a devoted environmentalist, and he wishes for a universal basic income to be set in stone. Musk self-described himself as being "half Democrat, half Republican," but that may be far from the truth.

The public has a hard time understanding Musk's political moves. He has an open aversion for unions, and he is clearly pro-business, but other than that, it gets a bit confusing. The most logical thing to assume is that his direct political involvement, through donations does not represent his beliefs. His main companies, Tesla and SpaceX, thrive with governmental largesse. The donations he's been making would just be so that he can keep benefiting from tax incentives and overturn dealer franchise laws. It's all business.

Furthermore, the causes that Musk defends are ones of world interest —like going green, saving the environment, helping humanity, etc. They want a piece of that good public opinion pie, and it's in their interest to support Musk's endeavors. A helping system that's usually a two-way street.

So is Musk a Democrat? A Republican? A Libertarian? Some ambiguous political mixture? Only he may know the answer to that, but to the public, one thing is clear. Musk is a businessman. And he will do whatever in order to help his ventures thrive.

Chapter 15: Religion

Being a tech guy and a science-oriented person, it's no wonder that he does not have a rich religious background or bond. He does not practice any sort of worshipping, and he is in a strong belief that science and religion could not coexist.

When he was asked if he believed that humanity was part of something greater, he responded, "Well, I do. Do I think that there's some sort of master intelligence architecting all of this stuff? I think probably not because then you have to say, 'Where does the master intelligence come from?' So it sort of begs the question. So I think really you can explain this with the fundamental laws of physics. You know its complex phenomenon from simple elements."[177]

It's not that Musk is an atheist or agnostic. He just has no link whatsoever with religion as he is focused on other things that require a more factual way of thinking. There is just no place for belief in his life right now. The same was with his childhood, despite speculations that make him out to be of Jewish background because of the name Elon—a Hebrew word for oak tree. But he got the name from his great grandfather, who was also not Jewish.

His faith lies in the abilities of the humankind. He believes that we, as humans, have the power to save ourselves from a possible extinction—caused by environmental factors or an AI supremacy. Musk is an ambitions risk taker, with a character that rubs many people the wrong way. He is by no means a saint or a person that has a god complex. He is just a guy with a vision and a greater purpose. Musk fights for humanity and its evolution, and that's enough. Whether he prays or not, whether he believes in a higher being that created the world and everything in it should not matter. His actions and his drive to help produce real changes in the world. Actions speak louder than words.

---

[177] 2008 OnInnovation.com, "Going to Mars with Elon Musk."

Chapter 16: Public Image

The media has a very polarizing opinion when it comes to Musk. Some love to hate him while others can't find any fault in his behavior or decisions. He is often praised for his achievements and toughness of character that paved the way for him becoming a billionaire, but he is also critiqued daily for his actions or his Twitter sprees. But at the end of the day, he has a loyal audience that supports him no matter what, and that will continue to do so in the foreseeable future.

Tham Luang Cave Rescue

At the end of June, the Wild Boars, a junior football team, along with their assistant coach went missing after they had set up to explore the Tham Luang Nang Non. It became apparent that the twelve boys and their supervisor remained trapped in the cave as it flooded due to abundant rains.

The case reached worldwide news outlets, and the Thailand Cave Rescue mission started. Thai rescuers received help from numerous experts, but the cave is so dangerous that even experienced divers were in danger of losing their lives. Thai Navy SEALs had a tough mission to pull out, and many plans and alternatives were taken into consideration. They began searching for the boys, and after more than a week of trial and effort, they managed to locate them, the miracle being that they were all alive, but between the rescuer's base and the boys, there were roughly four kilometers of dangerous terrain. Supplies and medicine were delivered while plans of extraction were in the works.

While this was happening in Thailand, in America another player was about to join the rescue efforts. Someone on Twitter asked Musk to help, and amazingly enough, he responded. He contacted the Thai government, and he ordered a team of his engineers from both SpaceX and the Boring Company to create a child-sized submarine that could help to safely get the kids out. Musk named the pod Wild Boar as a tribute to the football team and described it as being "basically a tiny, kid-size submarine using the liquid oxygen transfer tube of a Falcon rocket as hull."

By the time the mini-submarine was delivered, eight kids were already successfully retrieved. "Mini-sub is ready if needed. It is made of rocket parts & named Wild Boar after kids' soccer team. Leaving here in case it may be useful in the future," he posted on his Twitter. Because they were already so far with the rescue and due to the fact that the Wild Boar was seen as a risky alternative, the Thai rescuers opted to keep on getting the kids out, one by one with the help of a diver.

In the end, all thirteen victims were retrieved unharmed, albeit one diver lost his life during the mission.

Regarding Musk's involvement, some see it as a publicity stunt, as a bunch of engineers pointed out that the mini-submarine could have not been used as the cave was too tight for the pod. Others see it as Musk's genuine desire to help out in a dire situation where he was asked to intervene. It would not a be stretch to say that the promotional aspect might have motivated Musk to help, but as he has proved times and times again, he is a charitable person that strives to make the world a better place. It's very likely that he was interested because the cave rescue presented an issue that could have been solved by a technological approach, and he is always swayed by new opportunities to develop futuristic machinery. Maybe in the future, the Wild Boar prototype will be used in a similar situation after some tweaks and modifications.

The Joe Rogan Experience

In September 2018, Musk was a guest on the Joe Rogan Experience podcast in which he discussed several topics with the host for more than two hours. The comedian cherry-picked all of Musk's favorite topic, including artificial intelligence and technological advances.

He shared his thoughts on various issues, such as the negative effect of social media, signaling out the social platform Instagram especially: "People basically seem like they are way better-looking than they really are and they are way happier-seeming than they really are. If you look at everyone on Instagram, you might think, 'Man, there are all these happy, beautiful people and I'm not that good-looking and I'm not happy, so I must suck.'" He vented some about his harsh situation and how "nobody would want to be him." He reiterated that AI can be dangerous and could cause the doom of humanity and that he made a very controversial decision.

Rogan handed him a "blunt," which had a mixture of tobacco and marijuana, and after making sure it was legal, Musk took one smoke. The picture of him holding the blunt with a strange expression on his face became an internet sensation. Everybody started talking about the incident, most news outlets and internet personas blowing it out of proportion, affirming that he got high, that he was promoting the consumption of hallucinatory substances, and so on. For the media, it served as a juicy story and a testimonial that the billionaire was not in his right mind.

Musk declared, "I do not smoke pot. As anybody who watched that podcast could tell, I have no idea how to smoke pot, or anything," which would come as a valid explanation for his confused expression.[178] Many people that know Musk personally had described him as the type of person that does not even drink outside of events, so it's very unlikely that Musk would engage in pot consumption while also leading his companies with an iron fist. He just made a bad decision that the media "milked dry."

YouTube War: PewDiePie vs T-Series

Felix Arvid Ulf Kjellberg, widely known as PewDiePie, has the most subscribed channel on YouTube, and since the end of 2018, his fan base fought for the chance of maintaining his number-one title as the Indian channel, T-Series, is very close to surpassing him. It all became a digital war, as PewDiePie's fans started doing anything they could to help the Swedish man stay on top. The motivation is deeper than a matter of "who has the most subscribers." T-Series is a company that has many creators that post on their channel, while PewDiePie is managing his channel on his own.

---

[178] River Donaghey (2018), "Elon Musk Has 'No Idea' How to Smoke Weed, Says Elon Musk," *Vice.*

YouTube, since its early days, has been a platform for small creators that wanted to share their interests with the public. But as years passed and companies started seeing the potential behind the video platform, very few creators could rise up on their own, without having a studio or enterprise backing them up. PewDiePie is one of the few channels that come from a creator alone, to be so successful, and the YouTube community wants to make a stand: The most subscribed channel must belong to a creator. As it became clearer and clearer that at some point T-Series would pass a channel that posts only two videos a day, compared to the infinite resources that a company with multiple creators has, the goal changed. The fight is now to get PewDiePie's channel to 100 million subscribers before T-Series does so that first-time historical achievement would go to a creator.

On February 22, Elon Musk joined the PewDiePie team and hosted one of his most popular segments "Meme Review," which rates the latest internet jokes known as memes. "Elon Musk will host Meme Review" was a gig on Felix's channel for a while, and many of his fans wanted it to become a reality. Musk teased his fans by posting a picture of himself captioned "Host meme review?" in January. Needless to say, Musk has gained many fans for getting involved in such an Internet movement that mainstream media doesn't even cover unless it gives them the chance to slander in some way the digital sensation PewDiePie. It is unclear why Musk agreed to get himself involved. Maybe because he saw in Felix a person like him, that media loved to tear up, or maybe just because it seems fun for him. No one can know for sure what the charismatic man thought, but the YouTube community loves him for it.

Conclusion

There are many things that could be said about Elon Musk. He is impatient and driven. He likes to tweet. He never gives up on his dreams. He is a romantic at heart, and he has made some major changes in the aerospace and auto industries. He is a man that started from the bottom and built his own way up through hard work, ambition, and unshakable will. He made more enemies than friends in his road to greatness, and he is fine with that.

Elon Musk is a man that dreamed about changing the world since he was only a child, and he never swayed from his path no matter how many setbacks and financial problems he encountered. He is the kind of man that shatters conventional views and beliefs, and he crafts from scratch his own way of doing things.

As I've said before, Musk is the type of character that you either love or hate. There is no in-between. But no matter what the public thinks of him or how the media portrays him as a mad man, he keeps reaching new heights and changing the world little by little. No one can take that from him, and no one will. The world has yet to witness his greatest accomplishment, as he always strives for more.

Bibliography

Áine Cain, Inside the Turbulent Personal Life of Elon Musk, Who Called His Estranged Father "A Terrible Human Being" and Who Says He Must Be in Love to Be Happy, https://www.businessinsider.com/elon-musk-relationships-2017-11.

Aine Cain, The Relationship History of Elon Musk, Who Says He Must Be in Love to Be Happy, https://www.independent.co.uk/life-style/elon-musk-personal-life-love-relationship-wife-marriage-happy-talulah-riley-a8058611.html.

Alan Martin, 17 Things Elon Musk Believes, https://www.alphr.com/science/1001880/17-things-elon-musk-believes.

Alistair Charlton, How Does Tesla Autopilot Work, Is It Safe, and How Does It Compare to Truly Autonomous Cars? https://www.gearbrain.com/tesla-autopilot-technology-explained-2555878938.html.

Andy Patrizio, Dell Acquires Remote Management Firm Everdream, http://www.internetnews.com/bus-news/article.php/3711541/Dell+Acquires+Remote+Management+Firm+Everdream.htm.

Anthony Cuthbertson, Hyperloop: The 1,000 kph Race to Realize Elon Musk's Improbable Dream Heats Up in the Middle East https://www.independent.co.uk/life-style/gadgets-and-tech/features/hyperloop-one-uk-speed-updates-latest-elon-musk-virgin-hyperlooptt-dubai-a8312896.html.

Ashlee Vance, Elon Musk: Tesla, SpaceX, and the Quest for a Fantastic Future.

Austin Carr, The Real Story behind Elon Musk's $2.6 Billion Acquisition of SolarCity and What It Means for Tesla's Future–Not to Mention the Planet's, https://www.fastcompany.com/40422076/the-real-story-behind-elon-musks-2-6-billion-acquisition-of-solarcity-and-what-it-means-for-teslas-future-not-to-mention-the-planets.

Bill Bostock, Elon Musk's Reported Ex-Girlfriend Grimes Tweeted "Randomly, I am in China," on the Same Day He Launched His New Tesla Gigafactory in Shanghai, https://www.businessinsider.com/grimes-randomly-in-china-on-same-day-as-elon-musks-tesla-launch-gigafactory-2019-1.

Biography.com Editors, Elon Musk Biography, https://www.biography.com/people/elon-musk-20837159.

Buzz: Genomics Startup Halcyon Molecular tanks, https://www.fiercebiotech.com/r-d/buzz-genomics-startup-halcyon-molecular-tanks.

Calla Cofield, Watch Elon Musk React to Falcon Heavy Launch in Exclusive National Geographic Video, https://www.space.com/39655-elon-musk-falcon-heavy-launch-natgeo-video.html.

Chanan Bos, #Pravduh about #Tesla—3 Month Review of Top Publishers, https://cleantechnica.com/2018/12/08/pravduh-about-tesla-3-month-review-of-top-publishers/.

Claudia Assis, Tesla Stock Skyrockets after Legendary Short Seller Goes Long, https://www.marketwatch.com/story/tesla-stock-skyrockets-after-legendary-short-seller-goes-long-2018-10-23.

Drake Baer, The Making of Tesla: Invention, Betrayal, and the Birth of the Roadster, https://www.businessinsider.com/tesla-the-origin-story-2014-10.

Ed Oswald, Here's Everything You Need to Know about the Boring Company, https://www.digitaltrends.com/cool-tech/what-is-the-boring-company/.

Edoardo Maggio, Elon Musk Has Launched the "X.com" Website He Bought Back from PayPal Recently, https://www.businessinsider.com/elon-musk-officially-launched-the-xcom-website-2017-7.

Elizabeth Atkin, Elon Musk and Children—Family Facts, https://www.madeformums.com/news/elon-musk-children-bio/.

Elizabeth Lopatto, Elon Musk's Teslaquila Is Actually a Good Idea, https://www.theverge.com/2018/10/19/17995806/teslaquila-tesla-tequila-luxury-car-merch-elon-musk.

Elizabeth Lopatto, I Have a Boring Company Not-A-Flamethrower, https://www.theverge.com/2018/6/10/17445838/boring-company-flamethrower-elon-musk-tweets-party.

Elon Musk Reaches Thailand with "Wild Boar" Mini-Submarine for Rescue Ops, https://www.ndtv.com/world-news/thailand-cave-rescue-elon-musk-reaches-tham-luang-cave-in-chiang-rai-with-wild-boar-mini-submarine-f-1880575.

Elon Musk, https://twitter.com/elonmusk.

Eric Ralph, SpaceX's Partial Falcon 9 Landing Failure Could Delay Next West Coast Launch, https://www.teslarati.com/spacex-next-west-coast-launch-indefinitely-postponed-failed-falcon-9-landing/.

Everything about Elon Musk's Religious Views, https://blog.habrador.com/2014/01/elon-musk-religion-jewish.html.

Frank Jacobs, Welcome to Muskworld, a Map of Elon's Interests, https://bigthink.com/strange-maps/welcome-to-muskworld-a-map-of-elons-interests.

Graham Rapier, Tesla Is Surging after an Analyst Upgrade and Higher Spot on the Fortune 500 List (TSLA), https://markets.businessinsider.com/news/stocks/tesla-stock-price-surges-after-fortune-500-rank-analyst-upgrade-2018-5-1025066914.

How Was the Rivalry between PayPal and X.com before and after the Merger? https://www.forbes.com/sites/quora/2015/10/09/how-was-the-rivalry-between-paypal-and-x-com-before-and-after-the-merger/#1f6ec466154d.

https://www.bloomberg.com/research/stocks/private/snapshot.asp?privcapId=60169830.

https://www.crunchbase.com/organization/everdream#section-overview.

https://www.crunchbase.com/organization/oneriot#section-overview.

https://www.spacex.com/falcon9.

https://www.tesla.com/about.

Jack Stewart, Deep in the Desert: The Hyperloop Comes to Life, https://www.wired.com/story/virgin-hyperloop-one-engineering/.

James Dennin, There Were 3 Reasons Elon Musk's Boring Company Didn't Come to NYC, https://www.inverse.com/article/53321-the-boring-company-looked-into-a-desperately-needed-tunnel-in-nyc-report.

JEN WIECZNER, Tesla and 19 Companies Join the Fortune 500 for the First Time, http://fortune.com/2017/06/07/first-time-fortune-500-companies/.

Jessie Stephens, "It's Elon's World and the Rest of Us Live in it." What It's Like to Be Married to Elon Musk, https://www.mamamia.com.au/elon-musk-wife/.

Julia La Roche, Bloomberg News Pays Reporters More if Their Stories Move Markets, https://www.businessinsider.com/bloomberg-reporters-compensation-2013-12.

Kate Baggaley, Elon Musk's Hyperloop Dream May Come True—and Soon https://www.nbcnews.com/mach/science/elon-musk-s-hyperloop-dream-may-come-true-soon-ncna855041.

Kate Clark, Highlights from Elon Musk's Interview with Joe Rogan, https://techcrunch.com/2018/09/07/highlights-from-elon-musks-interview-with-joe-rogan/?guce_referrer_us=aHR0cHM6Ly93d3cuZ29vZ2xlLmNvbS8&guce_referrer_cs=cFhs9WV5DkLVuje8hB5jhg&guccounter=2.Kevin McCoy, Elon Musk Tripped Up by Legal Ruling over Tesla's $2.6B Acquisition of SolarCity, https://eu.usatoday.com/story/money/2018/03/29/elon-musk-tripped-legal-ruling-over-teslas-2-6-b-acquisition-solarcity/468627002/.

Lauren Weiler, A Timeline of Elon Musk's Marriage and Dating History, https://www.cheatsheet.com/entertainment/a-timeline-of-elon-muskss-marriage-and-dating-history.html/.

Marina Koren, A Triumphant Year for SpaceX, https://www.theatlantic.com/science/archive/2017/12/spacex-launch-falcon-heavy/549176/.

Mark Harris, How Elon Musk's secretive foundation Hands out His Billions, https://www.theguardian.com/technology/2019/jan/23/how-elon-musks-secretive-foundation-benefits-his-own-family.

Matthew DeBord, Here's Why Elon Musk Is Changing His Tune on Trump, https://www.businessinsider.com/why-elon-musk-is-changing-position-on-trump-2017-1.

Oliver McAteer, Elon Musk Has Launched a Mystery Website Called X.com, https://metro.co.uk/2017/07/14/elon-musk-has-launched-a-very-strange-website-called-x-com-6780414/.

Patricia Bauer, Zip2, https://www.britannica.com/topic/Zip2.

Peter High, Elon Musk-Funded XPRIZE Is One Step Closer to Ending Global Illiteracy, https://www.forbes.com/sites/peterhigh/2018/06/04/elon-musk-funded-xprize-is-one-step-closer-to-ending-global-illiteracy/#3a6d4cc34465.

Robert Ferris, Elon Musk May Actually Be Making a Website to Rate Journalists for Credibility and "Core Truth," https://www.cnbc.com/2018/05/25/elon-musk-may-actually-be-making-a-website-to-rate-journalists-for-credibility-and-core-truth.html.

Ryan D'Agostino, Elon Musk: The Popular Mechanics Interview, https://www.popularmechanics.com/space/moon-mars/a26513651/elon-musk-interview-spacex-mars/.

Sam Abuelsamid, Hey Elon Musk Fans, Don't Take It Personally, He Is Just Playing the Political Game, https://www.forbes.com/sites/samabuelsamid/2018/07/15/hey-elon-musk-fans-dont-take-it-personally-he-is-just-playing-the-political-game/#5bbf8eef7d30.

Samantha Chang, Amazon Welcomes Alexandria Ocasio-Cortez to "See for Herself" in Retort to "Dehumanizing" Worker Abuse Claim, https://www.ccn.com/amazon-invites-alexandria-ocasio-cortez-abuse-claim.

Sasha Lekach, Elon Musk Sued by SEC for Tesla Privatization Tweet, https://mashable.com/article/elon-musk-sec-tweet-lawsuit/?europe=true#fqrC6yohoiqd.

Sean O'Kane, Court Approves Elon Musk's Securities Fraud Settlement with the SEC, https://www.theverge.com/2018/10/16/17983032/elon-musk-sec-securities-fraud-settlement.

Shubham Goyal, What Did Elon Musk Do at PayPal/X.com? https://www.quora.com/What-did-Elon-Musk-do-at-PayPal-X-com.

Tesla Powerpack, https://www.spiritenergy.co.uk/kb-batteries-tesla-powerpack.

Tesla Powerwall: The Complete Battery Review, https://www.energysage.com/solar/solar-energy-storage/tesla-powerwall-home-battery/.

The Full Story of Thailand's Extraordinary Cave Rescue, https://www.bbc.com/news/world-asia-44791998.

Tim Bechervaise, Elon Musk: What the Tech Genius Is Teaching the Church, https://www.premierchristianity.com/Past-Issues/2017/March-2017/Elon-Musk-what-the-tech-genius-is-teaching-the-church.

Todd Haselton, Elon Musk: I'm about to Announce a "Neuralink" Product That Connects Your Brain to Computers, https://www.cnbc.com/2018/09/07/elon-musk-discusses-neurolink-on-joe-rogan-podcast.html.

Tom Huddleston Jr., How Elon Musk Founded Zip2 with His Brother Kimbal, https://www.cnbc.com/2018/06/19/how-elon-musk-founded-zip2-with-his-brother-kimbal.html.

Vijay Govindan, Bloomberg On Tesla—#Pravduh Gone Wild, https://cleantechnica.com/2018/09/19/tesla-bloomberg-pravduh-about-tesla/

Wikipedia.

Zachary Shahan, Remember the Tesla Death Watch? (Hahaha), https://cleantechnica.com/2017/07/28/tesla-death-watch-hahaha/

Zameena Mejia, Elon Musk 9 Surprising Facts about His Youth, https://www.cnbc.com/2018/12/20/teslas--elon-musk-9-surprising-facts-about-his-youth.html.

Made in the USA
Las Vegas, NV
24 May 2022

49293308R10094